The DK North Collection

Edited by
Dorothy T. Ratigan

First published 1994
Eagle USA
PO Box 48282
Seattle, Washington 98148

ISBN # 0-9629520-2-8

Printed in Hong Kong

Contents

Introduction

"For us, design represents one person's interpretation of what inspires their imagination, effects their senses and impresses them enough to share their vision with the world."

Diane Lincoln and Kim Barry are two new designers whose common passion for fashion and graphic design has brought them together as DK North to share their visions in the pages of this book.

Their studio is on a quiet tree lined street in Maine's largest city. Among brick sidewalks and shrubs it sits beneath huge trees that create a natural canopy of maple leaves. But, behind this unassuming, almost serene façade, are rooms filled with ambition, imagination and creative ideas. They are piled high with books, magazines and baskets of yarn for inspiration. Walls, tables and chairs become podiums for colorful swatches, swipes and story boards,

delivering classic statements, contemporary risks and casual chic. But as conversations of construction, color and technique swirl about the rooms, a wooden spinning wheel

Diane Lincoln - Kim Barry

and loom remain at the center of it all like guardians of tradition, offering a constant reminder of the origin of their craft.

Both Diane and Kim were introduced to knitting and fashion by their mothers at an early age. In fact, Diane vividly remembers her first attempt at knitting.

"I remember being fascinated by the way my mother could create mittens from a ball of yarn. She was very patient. After she showed me how to cast on stitches, I was anxious to begin. One day while home with a baby-sitter, I became determined to start knitting. But there were no needles to be found. So I sharpened two pencils and knit my first scarf. I was very proud of my first creation."

Crude but effective, it became a young girl's inspiration to master this new and fuzzy art form and to eventually gain an extensive knowledge of fibers through knitting, spinning and weaving.

For these young girls the mysteries of Nancy Drew were no match for the intrigue of all the famous names that filled the magazines with fashion. It was the beginning of a journey that would ultimately unravel the mysteries of their intense fascination with design.

"I think for both of us it has always been more than just looking good. And it wasn't so much a discovery of what was considered chic as it was a final understanding that designing was a mood, an attitude, a feeling, a creative interpretation of who we are or who we'd like to be. The materials we choose, the colors we select reflect how we feel inside. I guess for us, it's really quite simple. Good design means honest expression."

Fueled by desire on the wings of a dream, it was only a matter of time before their imaginations would literally take off from the runways of fashion in a flight that would ultimately bring them together to create designs of their own.

Inn By The Sea

Inn By The Sea

"There is something very exciting about successfully treating a classic design with dramatic flair or a theatrical touch using unique combinations of colors, patterns, textures, shapes and ornamentation. After all, this is what defines aesthetic direction.

"Each idea is like a flower that unfolds petal by petal until it emerges into the final design."

If there is a purpose to this book, it is to present you with an artistic proposal expressed in those colors, shapes and patterns imaginatively selected to flatter with confidence and style.

This Book is for you.

Yarn amounts in each set of instructions within this book are for the largest size unless otherwise indicated.

Gauge

The effort and time invested in knitting your design necessitates the importance of checking your gauge. It is imperative that you check your gauge before beginning to knit your garment. If the gauge is inaccurate, your finished garment will not be the expected size. The needle size given to obtain the correct gauge is only a recommendation. You may need to adjust the needle size up or down to achieve the correct gauge.

To check your gauge, knit a swatch using the yarn and needle size indicated in the pattern. For a color pattern, knit a swatch using the knitting technique suggested. Count your stitches and rows over four inches and if necessary, adjust the needle size accordingly.

Several designs in the book are sized by gauge instead of changing the number of stitches or rows. This demonstrates that the garment dimensions can be altered by changing the needle size.

Notes For Color Work

One square on the chart equals one stitch. Each pattern indicates which technique to use. Use the technique specified to achieve the best results with your finished garment.

Fair Isle Front View

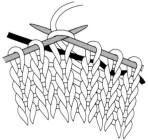

Fair Isle Technique

The Fair Isle technique is used when there are two or more colors worked over a repeating pattern in a row and when the number of stitches between colors is small.

Fair Isle Back View

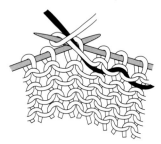

When working fair isle, strand the yarn not in use over no more than five stitches. If it is to be carried over more than five stitches, then weave the yarn over and under the yarn being worked.

Keep the strand fairly loose so that the work remains elastic. If the strand is pulled too tightly, the knitted fabric will pucker.

Intarsia Technique

Intarsia is used when there are isolated motifs on a background of contrasting color or when there are

Intarsia Front View

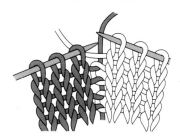

Intarsia Back View

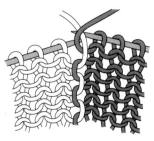

several blocks or patterns of color that are worked simultaneously. Carry separate bobbins of color for each individual motif.

To avoid bobbins from becoming tangled at the back of the work, you can use long lengths of yarn instead of individual bobbins. Cross yarns at each color interchange on the back side of work to avoid holes in the knitting.

Knitting Shoulder Seams

Place held left Back shoulder stitches onto a needle with tip at armhole edge. Place held left Front shoulder stitches onto a needle with tip at armhole edge. With right sides facing, hold both needles parallel with tips pointing in the same direction. *With a third needle, knit the first stitch of front needle together with first stitch of back needle and slip stitch made to right hand needle. Repeat from*. There are two stitches on right hand needle. Bind off one stitch. Continue in this manner until all stitches on both (each) needles are bound off together. Repeat for other shoulder.

Bind Off Loosely

For best results, bind off in pattern. Use larger needle to form working loop that is bound off.

Knitting Techniques

This prevents the bound off seam from being too tight and inflexible.

Mattress Stitch

Used for side and sleeve seams. With right sides facing, pick up the strand (bar) between stitches one edge stitch in from each edge of each piece as shown. Pick up one

Mattress Stitch Front View

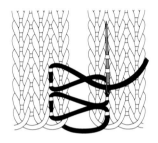

stitch bar on the first pass and then two stitch bars on each side after that. Then pull up on the yarn. Patterns will always match if worked in this manner.

Duplicate Stitch

This is an embroidery stitch that exactly copies the structure of a knit stitch.

Duplicate Stitch

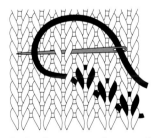

To work duplicate stitch, use the same weight yarn as the knitted fabric so that the background stitches are completely covered. Insert the needle from right to left through the base of the first stitch, then behind the base of the stitch above from right to left, then back

through the base of the first stitch and through the base of the second stitch to be covered.

Satin Stitch

Usually used for leaves. Worked across a given shape, the stitches may be straight or slanted. The thread should come up on one

Satin Stitch

side, lie smoothly on the surface next to the previous stitch and go down on the other side. Not to be used over large areas.

Chain Stitch

Bring the thread from back to front. Form loop. Insert the needle

Chain Stitch

where the thread first emerged. Gently, draw thread through. Work all stitches in the same direction.

French Knot

Bring the yarn from back to front. Wrap yarn around the needle 4 to 5 times. Insert needle back into

French Knot

the material slightly to the side of the emerging yarn. Work knots at random along Chain Stitch vine.

Stem Stitch

The thread may be held to the right or the left of the needle, but must remain consistent. Bring the thread from back to front. Insert

Stem Stitch

needle to the right of the emerging thread about a half stitch length and back into fabric at an angle for a broader stem stitch.

Abbreviations	
BO	bind off
cn	cable needle
CO	cast on
dec	decreas(e)(ed)(ing)
inc	increas(e)(ed)(ing)
k	knit
k1b	knit in back of st
k2tog	k2 tog
p	purl
psso	pass slip stitch over
rem	remaining
rep	repeat(s)
rev St st	reverse St st
rnd(s)	round(s)
RS	right side
sl	slip
ssk	slip, slip, k2tog
st(s)	stitch(es)
St st	stockinette stitch
tog	together
WS	wrong side
yo	yarn over

Rose Garden

Rose Garden

Sizes Small (Medium, Large)
Finished Chest Measurement:
44 (49, 55)"
Full Length: 34 (37, 40½)"
Sleeve Length: 13¾ (14¾, 16)"
Sleeve Width: 17½ (19½, 22)"

Charts: refer to pages 10–14

Materials
Mohair 90
(90% mohair, 6% polyester, 4% acrylic, 50gm skein = approximately 115 yds)
8 skeins color A, Snowdrift
1 skein color B, Rose Queen
2 skeins color C, Crimson Lake
4 skeins color D, Velvet Port
2 skeins color E, Creme de Menthe

Kashmir Mohair
(80% wool, 20% mohair, 50gm skein = approximately 105 yds)
3 skeins color F, Cardin Green

Impulse
(58% wool, 37% mohair, 5% nylon, 50gm skein = approximately 105 yds)
2 skeins color G, Raspberry
Body needle sizes under Gauge
Rib needle sizes 6, 7, or 8
Bobbins

Like an early morning mist, mohair creates a quiet diffusion of color, texture and shape for a look as soft and feminine as the sensuous scent of roses

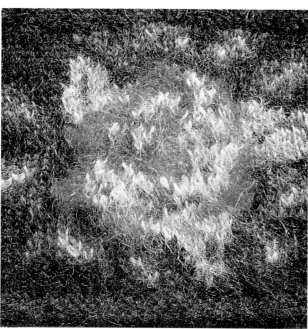

on a summer breeze. Gently flowing lines and festive, floral images exude a lavish appreciation for the sophisticated style and elegance of a classic design in this exquisite tribute to femininity.

Gauge
20 sts and 24 rows = 4" over colorwork using size 8 needles or size required to achieve correct gauge.
18 sts and 22 rows = 4" over colorwork using size 9 needles or size required to achieve correct gauge.
16 sts and 20 rows = 4" over colorwork using size 10 needles or size required to achieve correct gauge.

Pattern Stitches
1x1 Rib
Row 1: (RS) *K1, p1; rep from*.
Row 2: Knit the knits and purl the purls.
Stockinette Stitch
Row 1: (RS) Knit.
Row 2: Purl.
Honeycomb Border Pattern
Note: Slip all sts purlwise.
Rows 1 & 9: With color G, k19 sts.
Rows 2 & 10: P19 sts.
Rows 3, 5 & 7: *Sl1G, with color D, k5; rep from*, end sl1G.
Rows 4, 6 & 8: *Sl1G, p5D; rep from*, end sl1G.
Rows 11, 13 &15: K3D, *sl1G, k5D; rep from*, end k3D.

Rows 12, 14 & 16: P3D, *sl1G, p5D; rep from*, end p3D.
Intarsia technique (see Knitting Techniques) used throughout.

Note
Work individual roses and leaves with separate bobbins of color.

Back
With larger needles and color A, CO 36 sts. P1 row. CO 10 sts at end of row. Work Back chart, casting on 10 sts at the end of next 3 rows, 8 sts at the end of next 2 rows, 6 sts at the end of next 2 rows, 3 sts at the end of next 2 rows – 110 sts. Continue to work chart to beginning of neck shaping.
Shape neck: RS facing, work 38 sts in established pattern. Place center 34 sts on hold. Join new yarns. Work 38 sts in established pattern. Working both sides at the same time, at each neck edge on every other row, BO 5 sts twice. Work to end of chart. Place rem 28 shoulder sts on hold.

Left Front
With larger needles and color A, CO 11 sts. P1 row. Work Left Front chart as follows: Working in St st, at the end of every other row, CO 4 sts twice, 3 sts once, 2 sts 7 times, 1 st 8 times – 44 sts. Continue to work chart to beginning of neck shaping.
Shape neck: WS facing, BO 1 st on next row, then [every 4 rows, every 2 rows] 7 times, then every 4 rows once. Work to end of chart. Place rem 28 shoulder sts on hold.

Right Front
Work Right Front chart reversing bottom edge and neck shaping.

Sleeves
With smaller needles and color A, CO 44 sts. Work 1x1 Rib for 3½" inc 6 sts evenly spaced on last row – 50 sts. Change to larger needles. Work Sleeve chart, inc 1 st each end every other row 5 times, then every 4 rows 14 times – 88 sts. Work to end of chart or desired length. BO loosely.

Border
Knit shoulder sts of Front and Back tog (see Knitting Techniques). Work Honeycomb border pattern until piece measures full length around edging and neck of coat.

Finishing
Measure down 9 (10, 11)" from shoulder seam on Front and Back. Mark for underarm. Sew side seams matching patterns where possible from markers to bottom edge. Begin at right side seam, sew Honeycomb border in place along right front, around back neck, along left front, then around bottom to the beginning. Sew ends together. Set in sleeves between markers. Sew sleeve seams. Fold sleeve cuffs in half, turn to inside and sew in place.

Alternate color choice for garment: Black for main color.

Poppies and Iris

Poppies and Iris

Sizes Small (Medium, Large)
Finished Chest Measurement:
49 (53, 57)"
Full Length: 29½"
Sleeve Length: 18½"
Sleeve Width: 21½" (23, 24½)"

Charts: refer to pages 15–19

Materials
Crucci Baby Soft Mohair
(80% mohair, 18% wool,
2% nylon, 50gm skein =
approximately 109 yds)
7 skeins color A, Wilderness
1 skein color B, Khaki
2 skeins color C, Cyan
1 skein color D, Currant
1 skein color E, Lavender
1 skein color F, Sierra
1 skein color G, Cardinal
1 skein color H, Ocean
1 skein color I, Sunflower
1 skein color J, Melon
1 skein color K, Black
Needle sizes 8 and 10 or
size required to achieve
correct gauge.
Size 8, 24" circular needle
Bobbins
Six ½" buttons

Gauge
16 sts and 20 rows = 4" over
colorwork using larger needles

There is something mystical about the city of Florence. After a visit to the Galleria 'degli Uffizi museum to view the impressionist works of Cézanne, this designer was inspired by a field of poppies and irises against a background of ancient

ruins. Coaxed by the heat of the afternoon sun, their aroma crept through time and space to a kingdom filled with gentleness and beauty creating a souvenir of this one magical moment in time.

Pattern Stitches
1x1 Rib
Row 1: (RS) *K1, p1; rep from*.
Row 2: Knit the knits and purl the purls.
Stockinette Stitch
Row 1: (RS) Knit.
Row 2: Purl.
Intarsia technique (see Knitting Techniques) used throughout.

Note
Work individual color areas with separate bobbins of color.

Back
With smaller needles and color A, CO 98 (106, 114) sts. Work 1x1 Rib for 2½". Change to larger needles. Work Back chart to beginning of neck shaping. **Shape neck:** RS facing, work 35 (39, 43) sts in established pattern. Place center 28 sts on hold. Join new yarns. Work 35 (39, 43) sts in established pattern. Working both sides at the same time, at each neck edge on every other row, BO 2 sts twice, then 1 st once. Work to end of chart. Place rem 30 (34, 38) shoulder sts on hold.

Poppies and Iris

Left Front

With smaller needles and color A, CO 45 (49, 53) sts. Work rib as for Back. Change to larger needles. Work Left Front chart to beginning of neck shaping. **Shape neck:** WS facing, BO 1 st on next row, then 1 st once, 2 sts 5 times, 3 sts once. Work to end of chart. Place rem 30 (34, 38) shoulder sts on hold.

Right Front

Work rib as for Left Front. Work Right Front chart reversing neck shaping.

Sleeves

With smaller needles and color A, CO 46 (52, 58) sts. Work rib as for Back. Change to larger needles. Work Sleeve chart, inc 1 st each end every 4 rows 20 times – 86 (92, 98) sts. Work to end of chart or desired length. BO loosely.

Front Border and Neck band

Knit shoulders sts of Front and Back tog (see Knitting Techniques). With circular needle, color A, and RS facing, pick up and knit 92 sts along Right Front to beg of neck shaping, place marker, 15 sts along right neck edge, 12 sts along right back neck, 28 sts on hold, 13 sts along left back neck, 15 sts along left neck edge, place marker, and 92 sts along Left Front – 267 sts. Turn. Work 1x1 rib for 1½" and *at the same time*, inc one st each side of marker every other row. **Buttonhole Row:** RS facing, make 6 buttonholes evenly spaced along Right Front border as follows: Rib 5 sts, [k2tog, yo, rib 14 sts] 5 times, k2tog, yo, rib 5 sts. Work 1x1 rib for 3 more rows. BO loosely.

Finishing

Measure down 10¾ (11½, 12¼)" from shoulder seam on Front and Back. Mark for underarm. Set in sleeves between markers. Sew side and sleeve seams. Sew on buttons.

Alternate color choice for garment: Midnight, Ocean, Wilderness, Cyclamen, Sunflower, Currant, Khaki.

Oak Leaves

Oak Leaves

Oak leaves in warm earth tones, the very symbol of solidarity, take on a whimsical sense as they flit about in an autumn breeze.

Sizes Small (Medium, Large)
Finished Chest Measurement:
44 (48, 52)"
Full Length: 26"
Sleeve Length: 18"
Sleeve Width: 19½"

Charts: refer to pages 20–24

Materials
Eagle USA Glen Mist
(100% wool, 50gm skein
= approximately 113 yds)
12 skeins color A, Tartan
Green
6 skeins color B, Firecrest
2 skeins color C, Black
Currant
2 skeins color D, Burgundy
1 skein color E, Port Wine
2 skeins color F, Gorse Green
1 skein color G, Peat
Needle sizes 5 and 6 or
size required to achieve
correct gauge.
Size 6, 24" circular needle
Bobbins
Seven ¾" buttons

Gauge
24 and 32 rows = 4" over
colorwork using larger needles

Pattern Stitches
1x1 Corrugated rib
Row 1: (RS) K1F, *k1F, p1A;
rep from*, end k1F.
Row 2: *P1F, k1A; rep from*,
end p2F.

The neat, precise design of the border is like the crispness of the autumn air adding a divine plan to the random patterns of the season.

Stockinette Stitch
Row 1: (RS) Knit.
Row 2: Purl.
Seed stitch
Row 1: (RS) *K1, p1; rep from* over designated sts.
All subsequent rows - Knit the purls and purl the knits.
Intarsia technique (see Knitting Techniques) used throughout.

Note
Work individual color blocks with separate bobbins of color. Work all leaf motifs in Seed st.

Back
With smaller needles and color A, CO 132 (144, 156) sts. Work 1x1 Corrugated rib for 1½". Change to larger needles. Work Back chart to beginning of neck shaping.
Shape Neck: RS facing, work 56 (58, 60) sts in established pattern. Place center 20 (28, 36) sts on hold. Join new yarns. Work 56 (58, 60) sts in established pattern. Working both sides at the same time, at each neck edge on every other row, BO 8 sts 0 (0, 1) time, 6 sts 0 (1, 2) times, 5 sts 3 (3, 1) times, 4 sts 4 (2, 2) times,

3 sts 3 (5, 3) times, 2 sts 3 (2, 4) times, then 1 st twice. Work to end of chart. Place rem 8 shoulder sts on hold.

Left Front

With smaller needles and color A, CO 60 (66, 72) sts. Work rib as for Back. Change to larger needles. Work Left Front chart to beginning of neck shaping. **Shape neck:** WS facing, work first 24 sts and place on hold. At neck edge on every other row, BO 5 sts 0 (0, 1) time, 3 sts 1 (3, 2) times, 2 sts 7 (9, 13) times, then 1 st 11 (7, 3) times. Work to end of chart. Place rem 8 shoulder sts on hold.

Right Front

Work rib as for Left Front. Work Right Front chart reversing neck shaping.

Sleeves

With smaller needles and color A, CO 60 sts (all sizes). Work rib as for Back. Change to larger needles. Work Sleeve chart, inc 1 st each end every 4 rows 29 times – 118 sts. Work to end of chart or desired length. BO loosely.

Yoke

Knit shoulder sts of Front and Back tog (see Knitting Techniques). With circular needle, color A and RS facing, pick up and knit 1 row over 42 (45, 48) sts along right neck edge, 132 (138, 144) sts along back neck edge including sts on hold, 42 (45, 48) sts along left neck edge – 216 (228, 240) sts. Cut A. Slip 24 sts at each end on hold onto needle – 264 (276, 288) sts. With RS facing, work 8 rows of Front border and color blocks.
Shape yoke: With color B, dec as follows: work 18 sts, k2tog, *k2, k2tog; rep from* across color blocks, end k18 sts – 207 (216, 225) sts. With B, p1 row. RS facing, begin **Shoulder chart:** With color B, k3 (8, 3) sts, join color A. Work leaf motif 10 (10, 11) times, end k4 (8, 2). Work 16 rows of chart, dec 5 times within each leaf motif as indicated on chart. P1 row. With color B, *k1, k2tog; rep from* end k1 – 105 (111, 113) sts. Change to smaller needles and work 1" rib as for back. BO loosely.

Left Front Border

With smaller needles, color A and WS facing, pick up and purl 149 sts along Left Front edge. Work 10 rows Corrugated rib. BO loosely using both colors.

Right Front Border

Work 6 rows Corrugated rib. **Buttonhole row:** Beginning at bottom edge, rib 4 sts, *BO 2 sts, rib 20 sts; rep from* end last rep, rib 5 sts. Working in established pattern, CO 2 sts over BO sts in previous row. Work 4 rows Corrugated rib. BO loosely using both colors.

Finishing

Measure down 10" (all sizes) from shoulder seam on Front and Back. Mark for underarm. Set in sleeves between markers. Sew side and sleeve seams. Sew on buttons.

Embroidery

Split yarn into plies. Using 2 plies each 24" long, Chain Stitch (see Knitting Techniques) veins on seed stitch leaves. Use colors C, D, and G at random on B colored leaves. Use colors C, D, and E at random on A colored leaves.

Rose Garden Back

✓ = Cardin Green   ○ = Crimson Lake   ► = Creme de Menthe

● = Velvet Port   × = Rose Queen   □ = Snowdrift

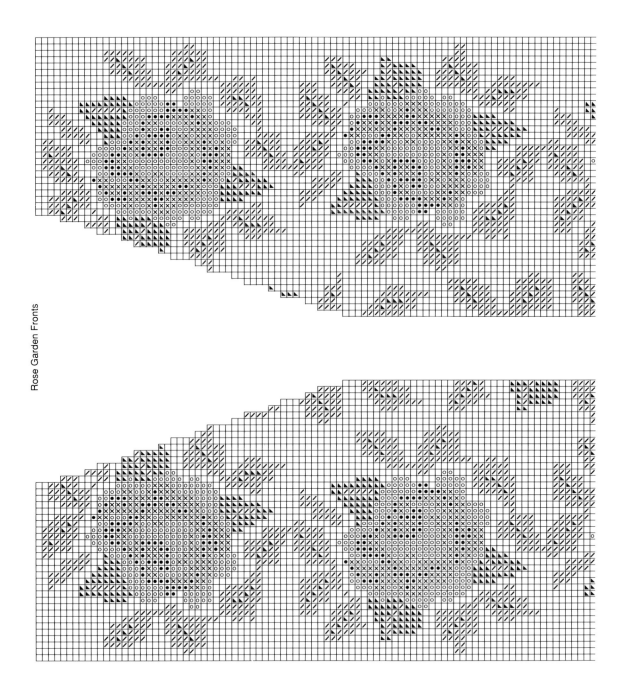

Rose Garden Fronts

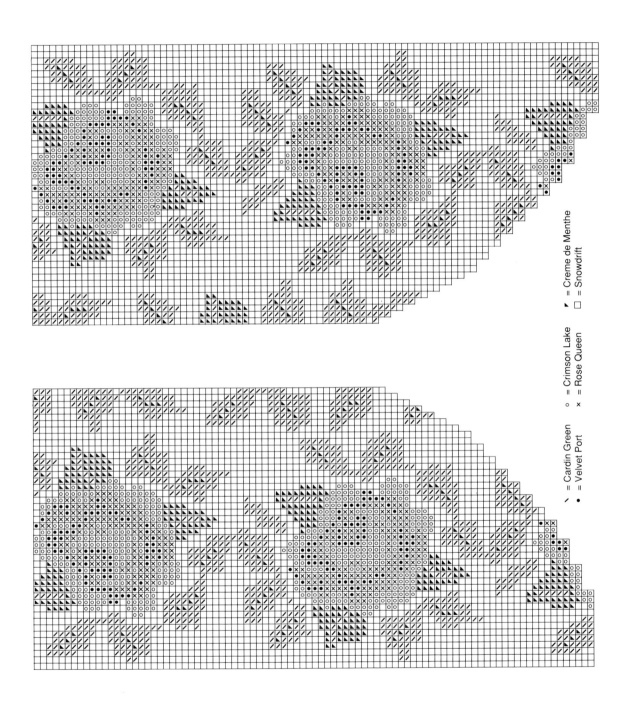

✓ = Cardin Green   ○ = Crimson Lake   ▸ = Creme de Menthe
● = Velvet Port   ✕ = Rose Queen   ☐ = Snowdrift

Rose Garden Sleeve

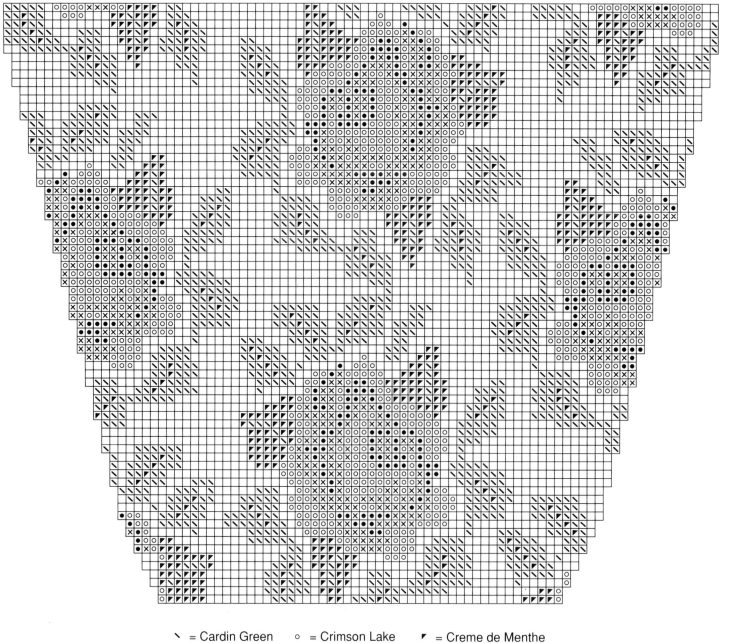

` ` = Cardin Green   o = Crimson Lake   ▼ = Creme de Menthe

● = Velvet Port   × = Rose Queen   □ = Snowdrift

Poppies and Iris Sleeve

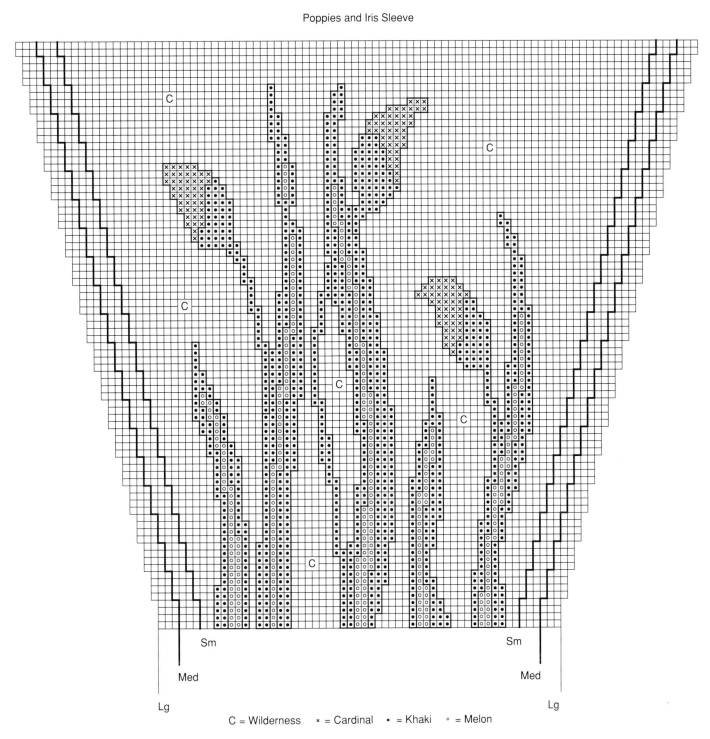

Sm

Med

Lg

Sm

Med

Lg

C = Wilderness   × = Cardinal   • = Khaki   ∘ = Melon

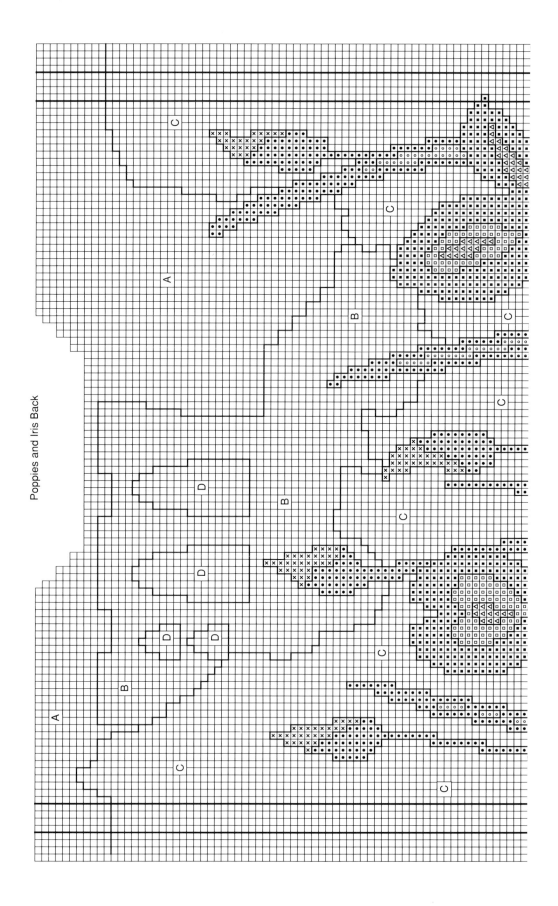

Poppies and Iris Back

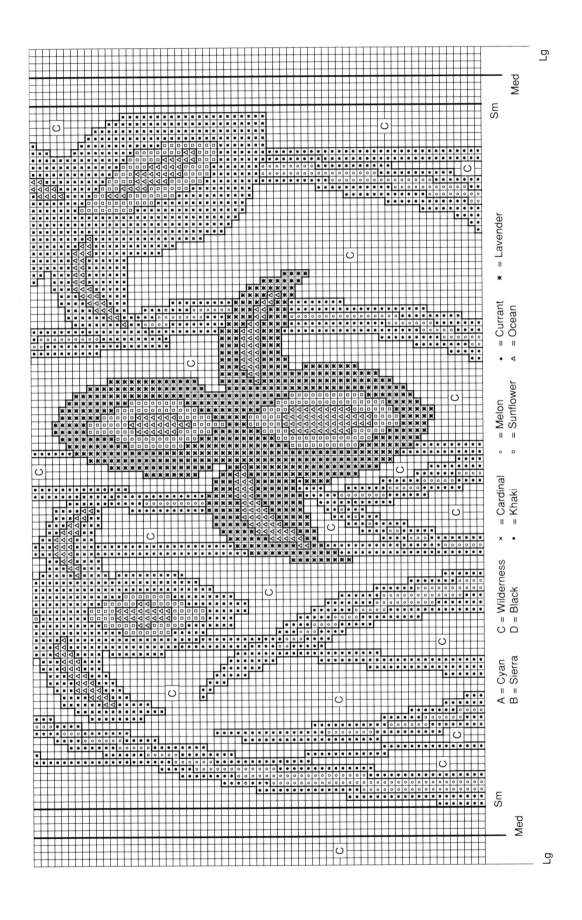

A = Cyan   C = Wilderness   × = Cardinal   ∘ = Melon   ＊ = Lavender
B = Sierra D = Black   ■ = Currant   ▫ = Khaki   △ = Ocean
                                              • = Sunflower

17

Poppies and Iris Fronts

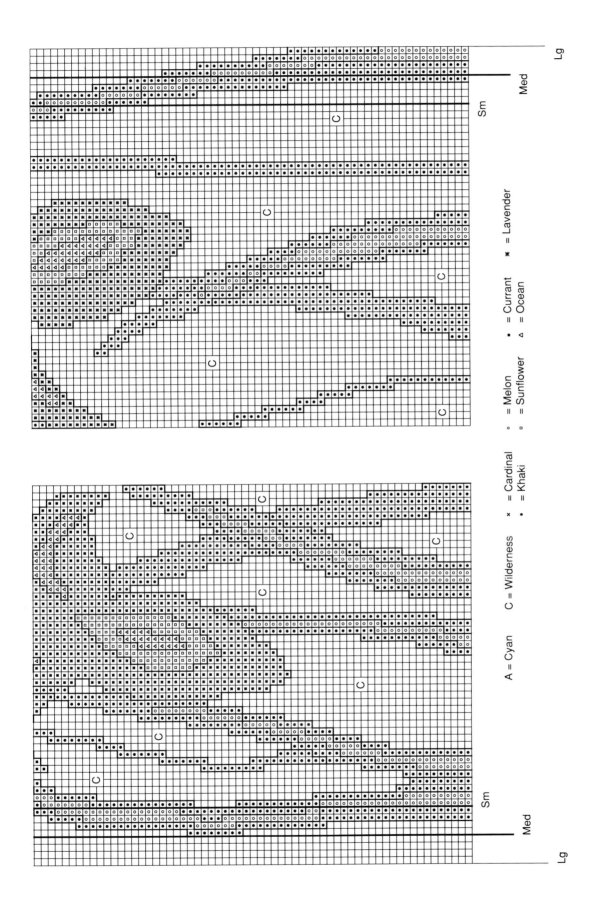

A = Cyan   C = Wilderness   x = Cardinal   * = Lavender
                                              • = Khaki
∘ = Melon   ▪ = Currant
□ = Sunflower   ▵ = Ocean

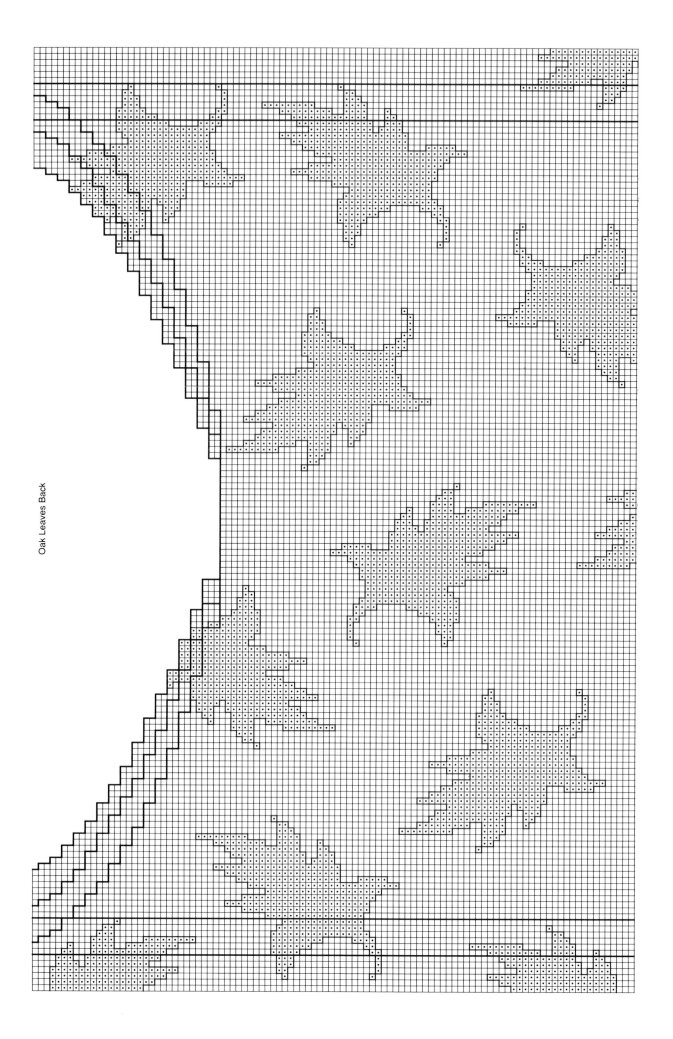

Oak Leaves Back

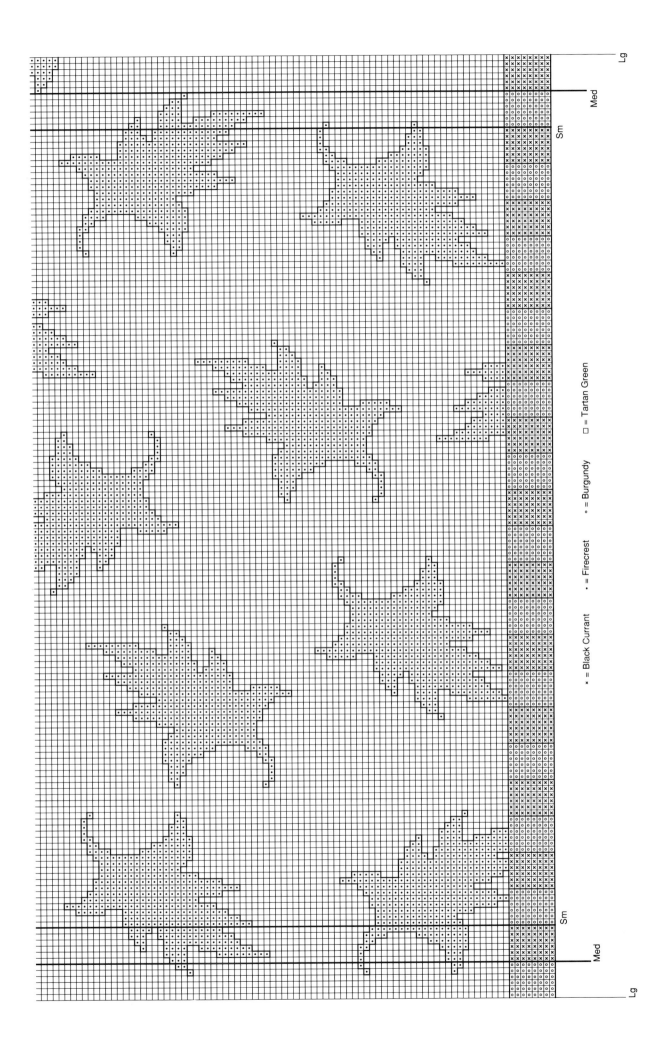

× = Black Currant   • = Firecrest   ○ = Burgundy   □ = Tartan Green

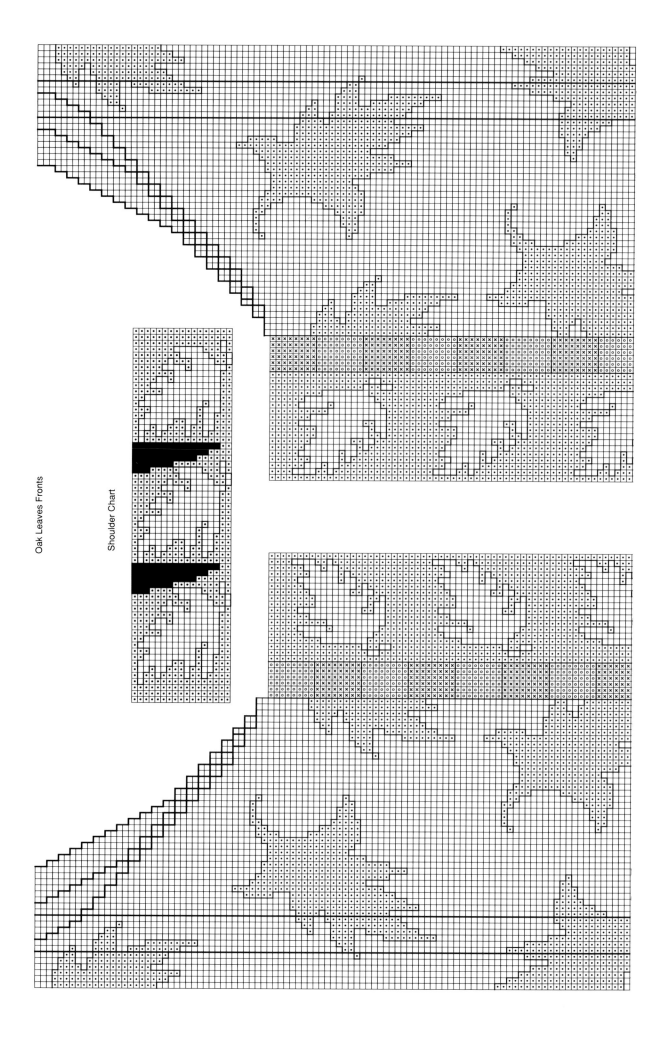

Oak Leaves Fronts

Shoulder Chart

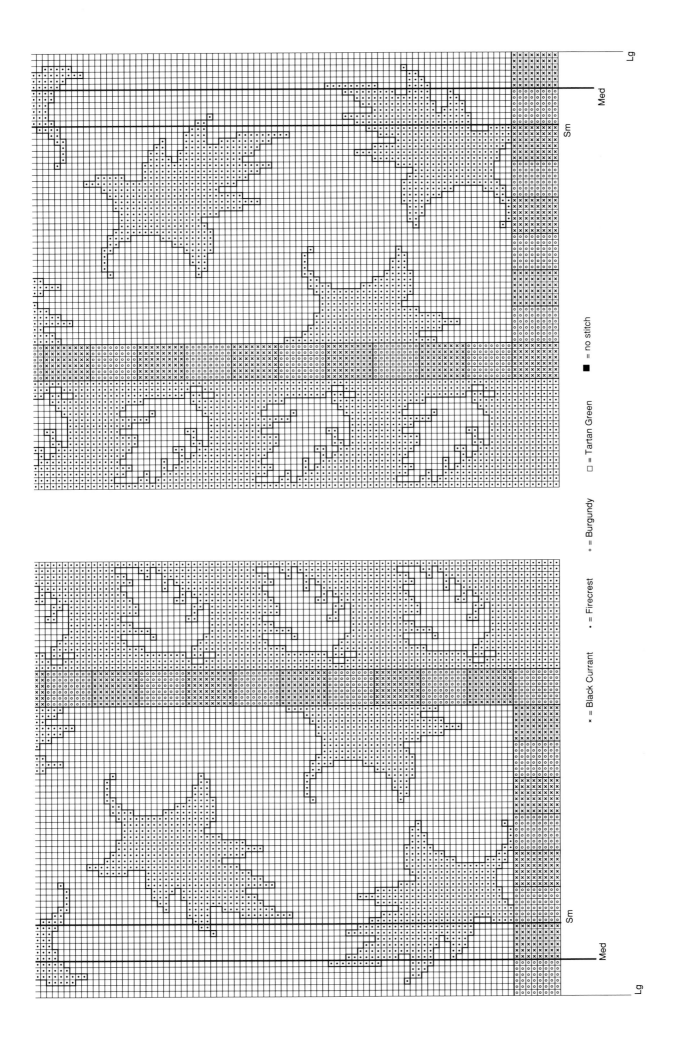

x = Black Currant   • = Firecrest   ∘ = Burgundy   □ = Tartan Green   ■ = no stitch

Oak Leaves Sleeve

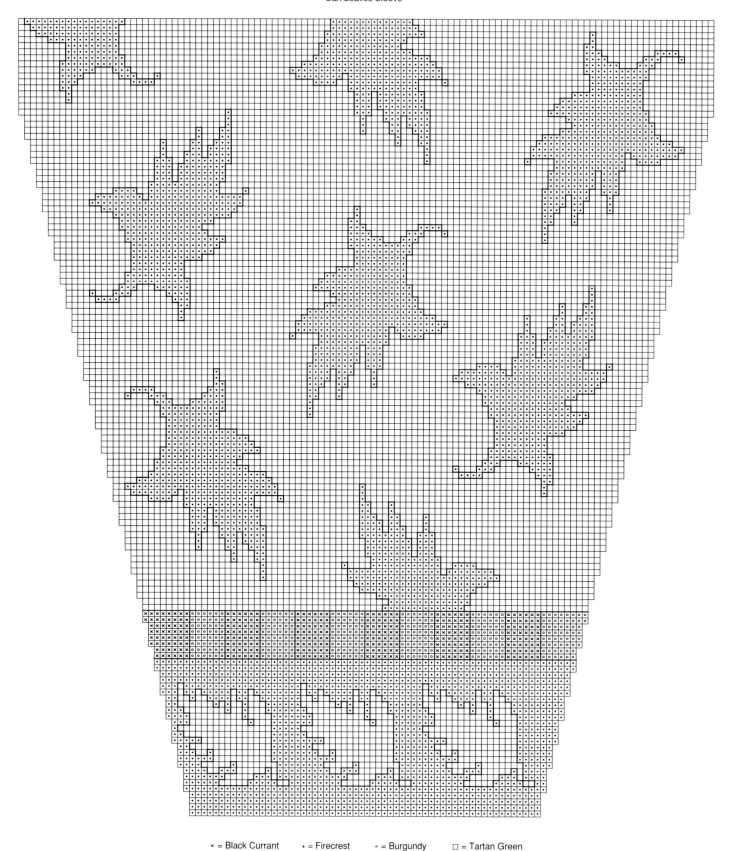

× = Black Currant   • = Firecrest   ∘ = Burgundy   □ = Tartan Green

Tartan

Tartan

Originally created to represent the Scottish clan, the tartan plaid of this cardigan is one clan destined to reveal the secret of casual chic. From the luxurious folds of its detailed shawl collar creatively inspired by a cathedral

Sizes Small (Medium, Large)
Finished Chest Measurement:
48 (51, 54)"
Full Length: 27"
Sleeve Length: 18½"
Sleeve Width: 22"

Charts: refer to pages 41–45

Materials
Eagle USA Accent Mohair
(78% Mohair, 13% wool,
9% nylon, 50gm skein =
approximately 120 yds)
6 skeins color A, Black
4 skeins color B, Lagoon
3 skeins color C, Pastel Blue
3 skeins color D, French Blue
Needle sizes 7 and 10 or
size required to achieve
correct gauge.
Bobbins
Four 1¼" buttons
Four ⅝" snaps

Gauge
16 sts and 20 rows = 4"
over colorwork using
larger needles

Pattern Stitches
Garter Stitch
Knit every row
2x2 Checked Rib (21 rows)
Rows 1 & 3: (RS) *K2D,
p2A; rep from*, end k2D.
Row 2: *P2D, k2A; rep from*,
end p2D.
Rows 4 & 6: *P2A, k2D; rep
from*, end p2A.
Row 5: (RS) *K2A, p2D; rep

window, to the elegant drape of its soft, sophisticated styling, it becomes the perfect companion for everything from sensuous silks to the common comfort of durable denim.

from*, end k2A.
Rep these 6 rows twice (18
rows total), then work:
Rows 19 & 21: *K2B, p2A;
rep from*, end k2B.
Row 20: *P2C, k2A; rep
from*, end p2C.
Front Border Pattern
Row 1: (RS) K3A, [k4C, k2A]
twice, sl1, k15A.
Row 2: P16A, [k2A, p1C,
p2D, p1C] twice, k3A.
Row 3: K3A, [k1C, k2D,
k1C, k2A] twice, sl1, k15A.
Row 4: P16A, [k2A,
p4C] twice, k3A.
Rows 5 & 11: K15A, sl1,
k15A.
Rows 6 & 12: P16A, k15A.
Row 7: K3A, [k4D, k2A]
twice, sl1, k15A.
Row 8: P16A, [k2A, p1D,
p2C, p1D] twice, k3A.
Row 9: K3A, [k1D, k2C,
k1D, k2A] twice, sl1, k15A.
Row 10: P16A, [k2A,
p4D] twice, k3A.
Stockinette Stitch
Row 1: (RS) Knit.
Row 2: Purl.
Fair isle Technique (see
Knitting Techniques) used
throughout body. Fair isle and
Stockinette stitch used on
front borders and collar.

Note
Short rows are worked at back
of collar to allow more ease
and a gentle shaping.

Tartan

Back

With smaller needles and color A, CO 94 (102, 110) sts. Work 2 rows garter st. RS facing, work 2x2 Checked rib for 21 rows. Purl back with color C. Change to larger needles. Work Back chart to beginning of neck shaping. **Shape neck:** RS facing, work 32 (36, 40) sts in established pattern. Place center 30 (30, 30) sts on hold. Join new yarns. Work 32 (36, 40) sts in established pattern. Working both sides at the same time, at each neck edge on every other row, BO 2 sts 3 times. Place rem 26 (30, 34) shoulder sts on hold.

Left Front

With smaller needles and color A, CO 40 (44, 48) sts. Work rib as for Back. Change to larger needles. Work Left Front chart to beginning of neck shaping. **Shape neck:** WS facing, dec 1 st every 4 rows 14 times. Place rem 26 (30, 34) shoulder sts on hold.

Right Front

Work rib as for Left Front. Work Right Front chart reversing neck shaping.

Sleeves

With smaller needles and color A, CO 38 sts (all sizes). Work rib as for Back for 9 rows only, then work Rows 19, 20 & 21. Knit 1 row with color C, inc 1 st each end of row — 40 sts. Change to larger needles. Work Sleeve chart, inc 1 st each end every 2 rows 4 times, [every 4 rows 4 times, then every 2 rows once] 4 times — 88 sts. Work to end of chart or desired length. BO loosely.

Left Front Border

With larger needles and color A, CO 31 sts (*see chart page 41*). Work 2 rows garter st. RS facing, rep 12 row Border pattern 6 times, then work Rows 1-6 — 80 rows. Reverse pattern placement and St st and begin to **Shape collar:** K15A, sl1, k2A, continue with Row 7 of Border pattern. Work Rows 8-12, then rep Rows 1-12, and *at the same time*, inc 1 st at each edge every other row 7 times, then every 4 rows 10 times — 65 sts. Work inc sts into Border pattern when appropriate. Work 2 reps of 12-Row Border pattern. **Short Row Shaping:** With color A, k32, sl1, k25. Turn. K26, p32. Continue in this manner, working short row shaping between each 6 rows of Border pattern 3 times. End pattern on Row 5. Place 65 sts on hold.

Right Front Border

Work as for Left Front reversing pattern placement and St st panel ending pattern on Row 11. With right sides of St st panel facing, knit and BO 33 sts tog. Turn work to RS and bring yarn to front. With wrong sides facing, continue to knit and BO rem patterned sts forming a garter ridge on front of work.

Finishing

Knit shoulder sts of Front and Back tog (see Knitting Techniques). Fold front borders in half and sew to front edging. Fold collar in half and sew shaped edge of collar to neck edge. Measure down 11" (all sizes) from shoulder seam on Front and Back. Mark for underarm. Set in sleeves between markers. Sew side and sleeve seams matching patterns. Sew on buttons on right front evenly spaced. Sew one half of snap on wrong side of right front under buttons and other half of snap on left front.

Alternate Accent Mohair color choice for garment: Magenta, Grape, Cyclamen, Plum Glitter.
*Alternate **Mohair 90** color choice for garment: Ebony, Silver Thread, Indigo Fashion, Fake Mink.*

Signature Cardigan

Sizes Small/Medium
(Medium/Large)
Finished Chest Measurement:
46 (54)"
Full Length: 28½"
Sleeve Length: 17½"
Sleeve Width: 19 (20)"

Charts: refer to pages 46–47

Materials
Eagle USA Unique 12 ply
(100% wool, 50gm skein
= approximately 81 yds)
10 skeins color A, Cream
9 skeins color B, Black
Needle sizes 6 and 8 or
size required to achieve
correct gauge.
Size 6, 24" circular needle
Bobbins
Cable needle

Gauge
18 sts and 24 rows = 4"
over pattern using larger
needles

Pattern Stitches
Garter Stitch
Knit every row.
Garter Stitch (in round)
Rnd 1: Knit.
Rnd 2: Purl.

The graphics of this dramatic cabled cardigan remind us not to get caught in the illusionary facade we accept as reality. For nothing is as it seems. Whether the

mood is colorful or black and white, it can be appropriately dressed to provide the perfect piece for the woman who knows where she is going.

Stockinette Stitch
Row 1: (RS) Knit.
Row 2: Purl.
2/2LC
Slip next 2 sts to cn, hold in
front, k2, then k2 on cn.
2/2RC
Slip next 2 sts to cn, hold in
back, k2, then k2 on cn.
Intarsia technique (see Knitting
Techniques) used on fronts
only.

Note
Work individual color
blocks with separate
bobbins of color.
Slip all markers on each
rnd of border.
Turn cables every 8 rows.

Back
With larger needles and
color B, CO 104 (122)
sts. Work in St st for
25½" ending on a WS
row. **Shape neck:** Work
31 (39) sts. Join new yarn.
BO center 42 (44) sts. Work
31 (39) sts. Working both
sides at the same time, at each
neck edge on every other row,
BO 2 sts twice. Place rem 27
(35) shoulder sts on hold.

Left Front

With larger needles and color A, CO 49 (57) sts. Work Left Front chart to beginning of neck shaping. **Shape neck:** WS facing, BO 6 sts. At neck edge on every other row, BO 4 sts once, 2 sts 3 times, then 1 st 6 times. Work to end of chart. Place rem 27 (35) shoulder sts on hold.

Right Front

Work Right Front chart reversing neck shaping.

Sleeves

With smaller needles and color A, CO 41 sts. Work 14 rows Garter stitch. Change to larger needles. Join color B. Work 6 rows of Border chart. Cut B. Continue with color A, inc 1 st each end on next row then every other row 3 (4) times, then every 4 rows 16 times – 81 (83) sts. Work until sleeve measures 14½" or 3" less than desired length. Join color B. Work 5 rows Border chart. Cut A. Work 12 rows in color B, inc 1 st every 4 (2) rows, 2 (4) times – 85 (91) sts. BO loosely.

Garter Stitch Border

Knit shoulder sts of Front and Back tog (see Knitting Techniques). Measure down 9½ (10)" from shoulder seam on Front and Back. Mark for underarm. Sew side seams matching patterns where possible from markers to bottom edge. With circular needle and color A, beginning at right side seam, pick up and knit 44 (51) sts across right bottom edge, place marker, k1, place marker, 92 sts along right front, place marker, k1, place marker, 20 sts along right front neck edge, 37 (41) sts along back neck, 20 sts along left front neck edge, place marker, k1, place marker, 92 sts along left front, place marker, k1, place marker, 44 (51) sts across left bottom edge, 93 (109) sts across back bottom edge, place rnd marker – 446 (480) sts. Work in the round as follows (see Note):
Rnd 1: *Purl to marker, inc 1, k1, inc 1; rep from* 3 times, purl to rnd marker.
Rnd 2: Knit all sts. Rep these 2 rnds 7 times. BO loosely in purl.

Finishing

Set in sleeves between markers. Sew sleeve seams.

Paleolithic

Paleolithic

Sizes Small/Medium (Medium/Large)
Finished Chest Measurement: 49 (55½)"
Full Length: 29½"
Sleeve Length: 18½ (19½)"
Sleeve Width: 20 (22¼)"

Charts: refer to pages 48–50

Materials
Crucci Sport Crepe
(100% wool, 50gm skein = approximately 65 yds)
15 skeins color A, Rust
Unique 12 ply
(100% wool, 50gm skein = approximately 83 yds)
4 skeins color B, Mash
2 skeins color C, Purple
1 skein color D, Petral
1 skein color E, Old Gold
Needle sizes 8 and 9 or size required to achieve correct gauge.
Size 8, 24" circular needle
Bobbins
Eight ½" buttons

Gauge
17 sts and 22 rows = 4" over colorwork using larger needles

Pattern Stitches
Garter stitch
Knit every row.

Inspired by a strong sense of history, primitive figures dance across a rust colored background as the original drawings must have danced in the light

of the artist's fire. Fixed in yarn as they were in time, they depict the body, mind and spirit of some ancient artist whose primal need for creative expression finds another voice in a more contemporary setting.

2x2 Corrugated Rib
Row 1: (RS) *K2B, p2C; rep from*, end k2B.
Row 2: *P2B, k2C; rep from*, end p2B.
Stockinette Stitch
Row 1: (RS) Knit.
Row 2: Purl.
Intarsia Technique (see Knitting Techniques) used throughout.

Note
Work individual color blocks with separate bobbins of color.

Back
With smaller needles and color C, CO 98 (110) sts. Work 3 rows garter stitch. Join color B and work 2x2 Corrugated rib for 3" inc 6 (8) sts on last row of rib – 104 (118) sts. Change to larger needles. Work Back chart to beginning of neck shaping. **Shape neck:** RS facing, work 37 (44) sts in established pattern. Place center 30 sts on hold. Work 37 (44) sts in established pattern. Working both sides at the same time, at each neck edge on every other row, BO 2 sts twice. Work to end of chart. Place rem 33 (40) shoulder sts on hold.

Left Front

With smaller needles and color C, CO on 46 (52) sts. Work rib as for Back inc 3 (4) sts on last row of rib – 49 (56) sts. Change to larger needles. Work Left Front chart to beginning of neck shaping. **Shape neck:** WS facing, BO 5 sts. At neck edge on every other row, BO 3 sts once, 2 sts twice, then 1 st 4 times. Work to end of chart. Place rem 33 (40) shoulder sts on hold.

Right Front

Work rib as for Left Front. Work Right Front chart reversing neck shaping.

Sleeves

With smaller needles and color C, CO 49 sts (both sizes). Work rib as for Back. Change to larger needles. Work Sleeve chart inc 1 st each end [every 6 rows, then every 4 rows] 6 (2) times, [every 4 rows, then every 2 rows] 0 (7) times, then every 4 rows 6 (5) times – 85 (95) sts. BO loosely.

Front Border and Neck band

Knit shoulder sts of Front and Back tog (see Knitting Techniques). With circular needle, color C, and RS facing, pick up and knit 116 sts along right front, place marker, 74 sts along neck edge, place marker, then 116 sts along left front – 306 sts. Purl 1 row. Follow Border Chart, inc 1 st each side of marker in color C every other row 4 times and *at the same time*, on Row 4, work

Buttonhole row. WS facing, work in established pattern to second neck marker. Work 5 sts, *BO 2 sts, work 13 sts in pattern; rep from* end last rep, work 5 sts in pattern. Next row: Working in established pattern, CO 2 sts over BO sts in previous row. Continue to follow chart and beginning on Row 11, dec 1 st each side of every marker every other row 4 times. Fold facing to inside and slip stitch in place.

Finishing

Measure down 10 (11)" from shoulder seam on Front and Back. Mark for underarm. Set in sleeves between markers. Sew side and sleeve seams matching patterns. Sew on buttons.

Jester

Jester

Inspired by the unpredictability of the Jester and his court, the colors and patterns criss and cross like the Jester moving from one trick to the next

Sizes Small (Medium, Large)
Finished Chest Measurement:
44 (48, 52)"
Full Length: 27½"
Sleeve Length: 18"
Sleeve Width: 20¼ (21¼, 22¼)"

Charts: refer to pages 51–55

Materials
Eagle USA Unique 12 ply
(100% wool, 50gm skein
= approximately 82 yds)
8 skeins color A, Black
4 skeins color B, White
2 skeins color C, Red
2 skeins color D, Cranberry
2 skeins color E, Roman
Purple
Needle sizes 6 and 8 or
size required to achieve
correct gauge.
Size 7, 16" circular needle
Bobbins

Gauge
16 sts and 22 rows = 4"
over colorwork using larger
needles

Pattern Stitches
1x1 Corrugated rib
Row 1: (RS) *K1B, p1A; rep
from*, end k1B.
Row 2: *P1B, k1A; rep from*,
end p1B.

catching us off-guard with a sense of drama and comedic timing. Bold graphics in black and white that begin the Jester's tale, suddenly burst into color as the punch line is delivered.

Stockinette stitch
Row 1: (RS) Knit.
Row 2: Purl.
Seed stitch
Row 1: (RS) *K1, p1; rep
from* over designated sts.
All subsequent rows - Knit the
purls and purl the knits.
Intarsia technique (see Knitting
Techniques) is used for color
blocks. Seed st is used for
vertical color A panels.

Note
On sleeve chart, there are
panels of color B in St st
with a diagonal purl st,
and panels of color A in
Seed st. Work all sts as
indicated on the chart.

Back
With smaller needles and
color B, CO 91 (97,
105) sts. Work 1x1
Corrugated rib for 2".
Change to larger needles.
Work Back chart to beginning
of neck shaping. **Shape neck:**
RS facing, work 39 (42, 46)
sts in established pattern.
Place center 13 sts on hold.
Join new yarns. Work 39 (42,
46) sts in established pattern.

Working both sides at the same time, at each neck edge on every other row, BO 3 sts twice, then 2 sts twice. Work to end of chart. Place rem 29 (32, 36) shoulder sts on hold.

Front

Work as for Back to beginning of Front neck shaping. **Shape neck:** RS facing, work 40 (43, 47) sts in established pattern. Place center 11 sts on hold. Join new yarns. Work 40 (43, 47) sts in established pattern. Working both sides at the same time, at each neck edge on every other row, BO 4 sts twice, 2 sts once, then 1 st once. Work to end of chart. Place rem 29 (32, 36) shoulder sts on hold.

Sleeves

With smaller needles and color B, CO 39 (43, 47) sts. Work rib as for Back. Change to larger needles. Work Sleeve chart, inc 1 st each end every 4 rows 21 times – 81 (85, 89) sts. Work to end of chart or desired length. BO loosely.

Neck band

Knit shoulder sts of Front and Back tog (see Knitting Techniques). With circular needle and color D, pick up and knit 72 sts around neck including sts on hold. Work Collar pattern repeat (see chart on page 51) in St st over next 11 rows. With color A, work 1x1 rib for 10 rows. BO loosely in rib. Fold to inside and slip stitch in place at base of neckline.

Finishing

Measure down $10^{1}/_{4}$ ($10^{3}/_{4}$, $11^{1}/_{4}$)" from shoulder seam on Front and Back. Mark for underarm. Set in sleeves between markers. Thread tapestry needle with color A. Strand A in a zig-zag diagonal direction through the purl bumps on color B panels on both sleeves. Secure ends. Sew side and sleeve seams matching patterns.

Alternate color choice for garment: Rose, Spruce, Lupine, Lilac, Black.

Shawl Collar Cardigan

Shawl Collar Cardigan

This classic, but non-traditional, over-sized sweater is the perfect weekend companion for spending time with friends or your favorite

book. Wrapping yourself in the magnificent shawl collar is like nesting in the folds of a luxurious mohair blanket filled with quiet, recuperative powers.

Sizes Small (Medium, Large)
Finished Chest Measurement:
48 (52, 56)"
Full Length: 30"
Sleeve Length: 18"
Sleeve Width: 22"

Materials
Crucci Brambles
(49% wool, 47% Mohair, 4% nylon, 50gm skein = approximately 74 yds)
22 skeins, Teal
Needle sizes 7 and 9 or size required to achieve correct gauge.
Four 1" buttons

Gauge
16 sts and 22 rows = 4" over St st using larger needles

Pattern Stitches
1x1 Rib
Row 1: (RS) *K1, p1; rep from*.
Row 2: Knit the knits and purl the purls.
Stockinette Stitch
Row 1: (RS) Knit.
Row 2: Purl.
Seeded Rib (multiple of 4+1)
Row 1: (RS) *K2, p2; rep from*, end k1.
Row 2: Rep Row 1.

Back
With smaller needles, CO 98 (106, 114) sts. Work 1x1 Rib for 2". Change to larger needles. Work in St st until piece measures 29" from beg.
Shape neck: RS facing, work 39 (43, 47) sts in established pattern. Join new yarn. BO center 20 sts. Work 39 (43, 47) sts in established pattern. Working both sides at the same time, at each neck edge on every other row, BO 4 sts once, 2 sts once, then 1 st once. Place rem 32 (36, 40) shoulder sts on hold.

Pocket Linings
Make 2. With larger needles, CO 22 sts. Work in St st for 5½". Place sts on spare needle.

Left Front
With smaller needles, CO 55 (59, 63) sts. Work rib as for Back. RS facing, change to larger needles and St st. K1 row, casting on 5 sts at end of row (front facing) – 60 (64, 68) sts. P1 row. Knit to last 6 sts, sl1 (turning ridge), k5. Continue to work slip-st facing and St st body until piece measures 5½" above rib.

Shawl Collar Cardigan

Insert pocket lining: RS facing, k16 (20, 22) sts, place next 22 sts on hold, k22 sts of pocket lining from spare needle, k16 (16, 18) sts, sl1, k5. Continue in established pattern until piece measures 16" from beg. **Shape neck:** WS facing, BO 17 sts loosely, purl to end. Working in St st only, dec 1 st at neck edge every 6 rows 11 times. Work until piece measures same length as Back at shoulder. Place rem 32 (36, 40) shoulder sts on hold.

Right Front

With smaller needles, CO 55 (59, 63) sts. Work rib as for Back, ending with WS facing. CO 5 sts. Change to larger needles. K5, sl1, knit to end of row. Work in established pattern until piece measures 1" above 5 cast-on sts.

Buttonhole row: RS facing, *k2, BO 2 sts, k1, sl1, k1, BO 2 sts, knit to end of row. Purl to last 9 sts, CO 2, p3, CO 2, p2. Continue to work slip-st facing and St st body for 4" end RS facing. Rep from* twice and *at the same time*, when piece measures 5½", insert pocket lining as for Left Front. Work until piece measures 15", work last buttonhole. Continue to work slip-st facing and St st body for 1" above last buttonhole. RS facing, BO 17 sts loosely, knit to end. Shape neck as for Left Front reversing shaping.

Sleeves

With smaller needles, CO 40 sts (all sizes). Work rib as for Back. Change to larger needles and work in St st, inc 1 st each end every other row 4 times, then every 4 rows 20 times – 88 sts. Work even until piece measures 18" from beg or desired length. BO loosely.

Collar

With smaller needles, CO 45 sts (all sizes) and work Seeded rib pattern. Inc 1 st in pattern at each end every 6 rows 14 times – 73 sts. Work even in established pattern for 11". Dec 1 st in pattern at each end on next row, then every 6 rows 14 times – 45 sts. BO loosely.

Finishing

Knit shoulder sts of Front and Back tog (see Knitting Techniques). Fold front facings along slip-st ridge to inside and sew in place. Measure down 11" (all sizes) from shoulder seam on Front and Back. Mark for underarm. Set in sleeves between markers. Fold collar in half. Sew shaped edge of collar to body around neck edge. Sew ends of collar to tops of front bands easing sts to fit. Slip 22 pocket sts on hold to smaller needles and work 1x1 rib for 1". BO in rib. Sew pocket linings and pocket bands in place. Sew side and sleeve seams. Sew on buttons.

Alternate color choices for garment: Khaki, Terracotta.

Tartan Left Front Border and half of Collar.
Reverse Pattern placement for Right Front.

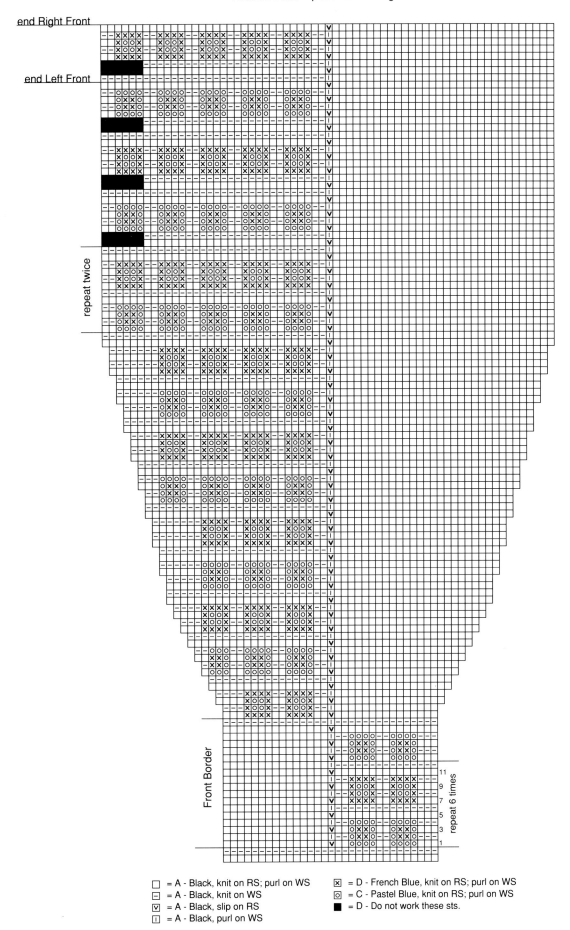

end Right Front

end Left Front

repeat twice

Front Border

11
9
7
5
3
1

repeat 6 times

☐ = A - Black, knit on RS; purl on WS
⊟ = A - Black, knit on WS
☑ = A - Black, slip on RS
Ⅱ = A - Black, purl on WS

☒ = D - French Blue, knit on RS; purl on WS
◉ = C - Pastel Blue, knit on RS; purl on WS
■ = D - Do not work these sts.

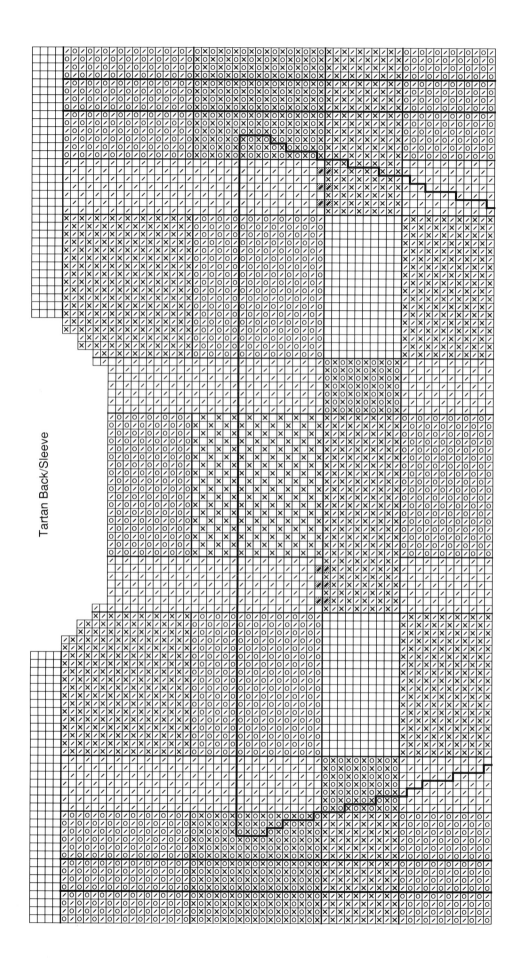

Tartan Back/Sleeve

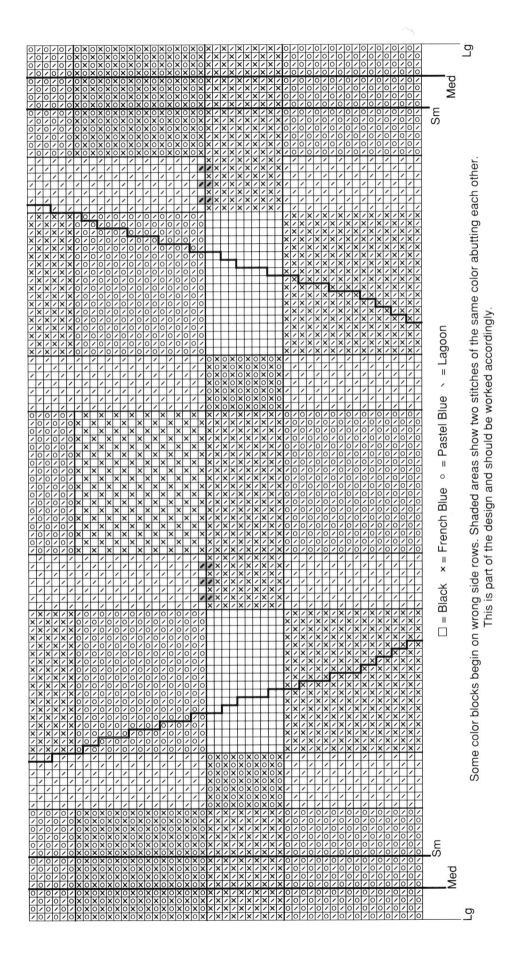

□ = Black   × = French Blue   ○ = Pastel Blue   ✓ = Lagoon

Some color blocks begin on wrong side rows. Shaded areas show two stitches of the same color abutting each other.
This is part of the design and should be worked accordingly.

43

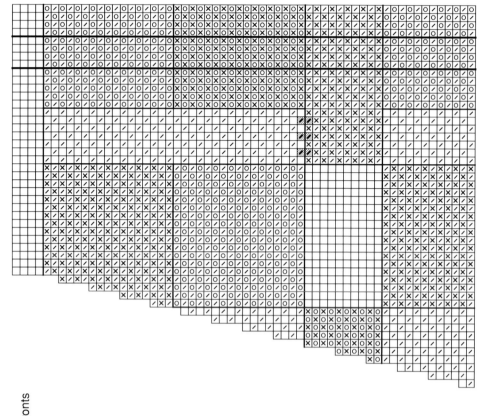

Tartan Fronts

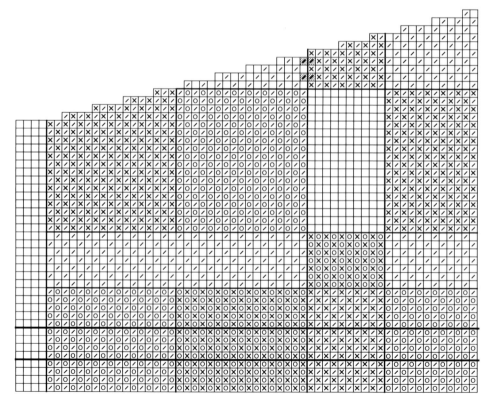

44

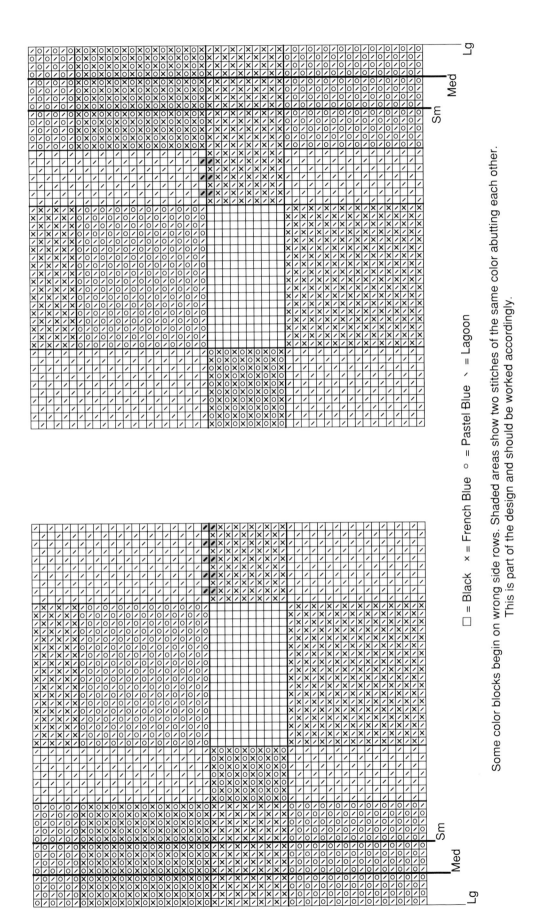

□ = Black   × = French Blue   ○ = Pastel Blue   ✓ = Lagoon

Some color blocks begin on wrong side rows. Shaded areas show two stitches of the same color abutting each other. This is part of the design and should be worked accordingly.

45

Signature Cardigan

Sleeve Border

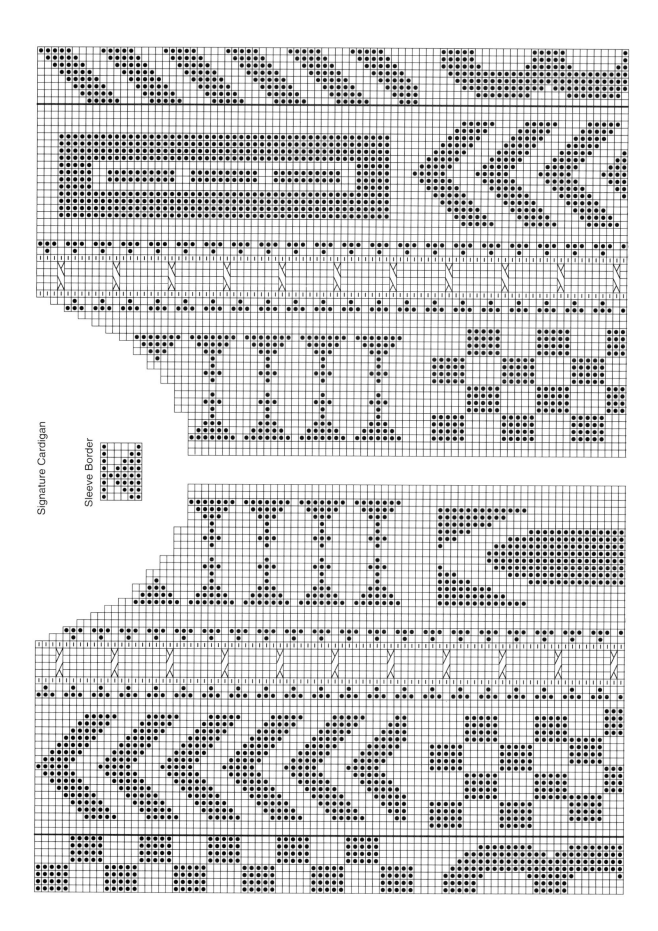

Med/Lg

Sm/Med

Med/Lg

Sm/Med

• = Black □ = White — = purl on RS; knit on WS

⧅ =2/2 LC. Slip 2 to cn to front, k2, k2 on cn.

⧄ =2/2 RC. Slip 2 to cn to back, k2, k2 on cn.

47

Paleolithic Back/Fronts

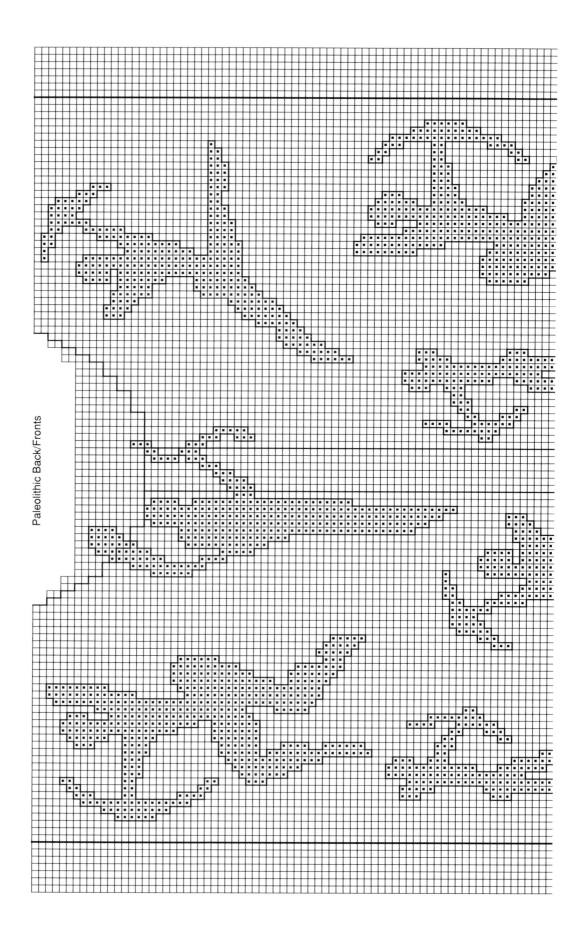

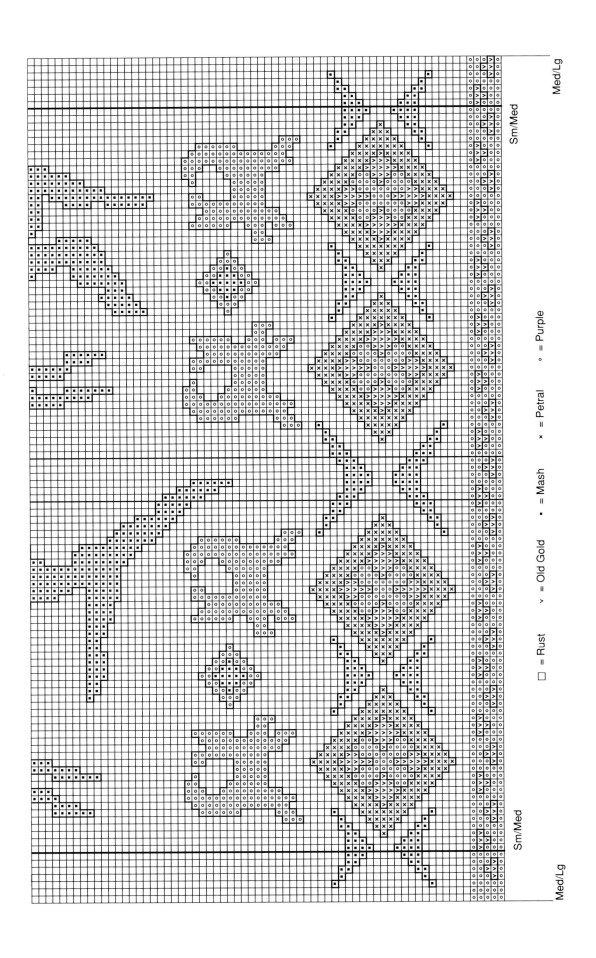

Med/Lg

Sm/Med

☐ = Rust   ∨ = Old Gold   • = Mash   × = Petral   ∘ = Purple

Sm/Med

Med/Lg

49

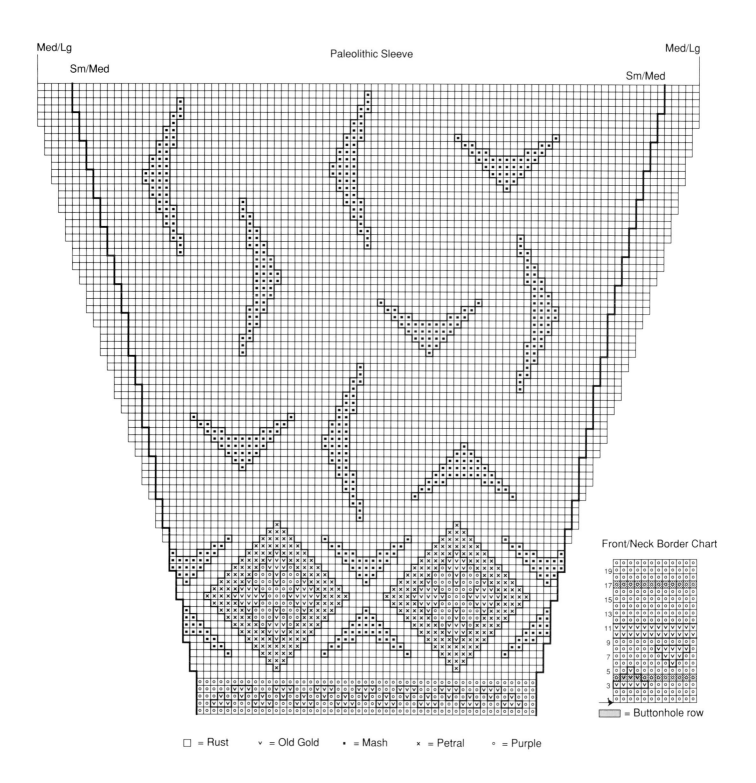

Med/Lg

Sm/Med

Med/Lg

Sm/Med

Front/Neck Border Chart

19
17
15
13
11
9
7
5
3

= Buttonhole row

□ = Rust   v = Old Gold   ▪ = Mash   x = Petral   ○ = Purple

50

Jester Sleeve

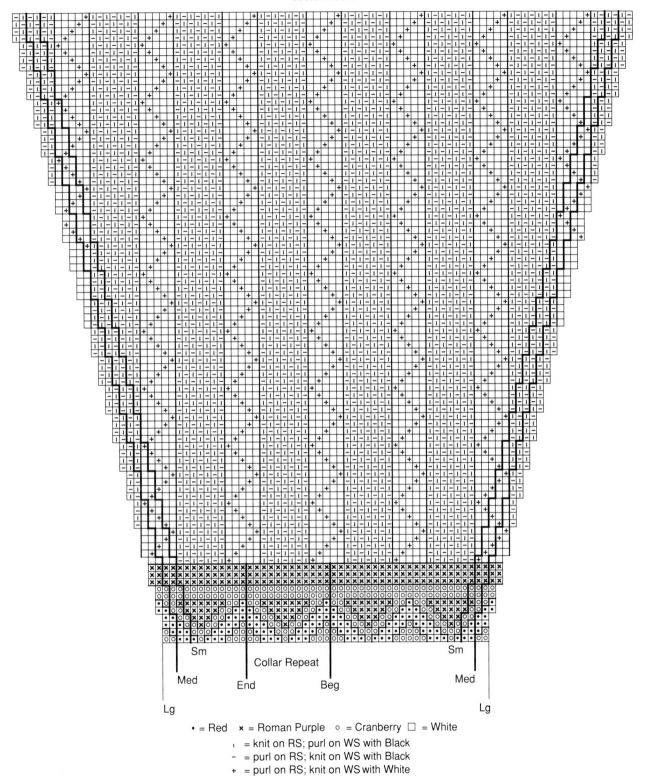

Sm

Collar Repeat

Sm

Med

End   Beg

Med

Lg

Lg

• = Red   ✗ = Roman Purple   ○ = Cranberry   □ = White

ı = knit on RS; purl on WS with Black

- = purl on RS; knit on WS with Black

+ = purl on RS; knit on WS with White

51

Jester Back

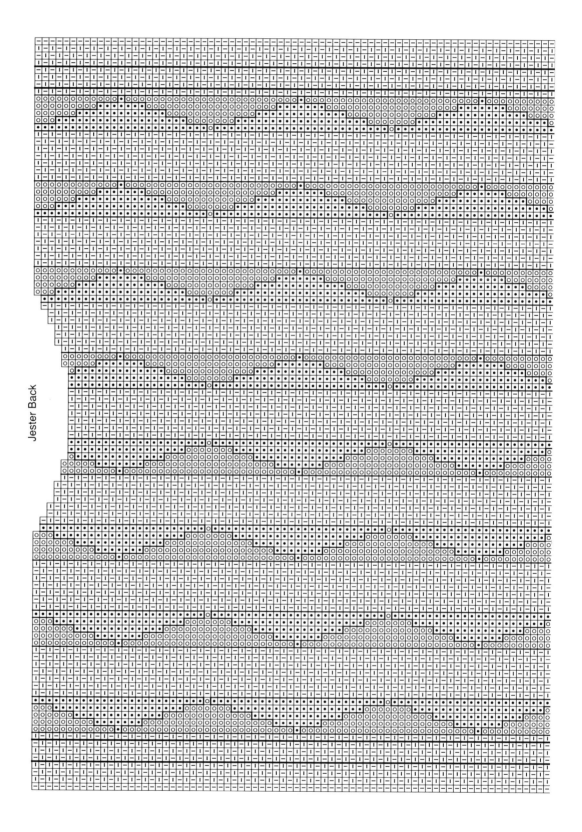

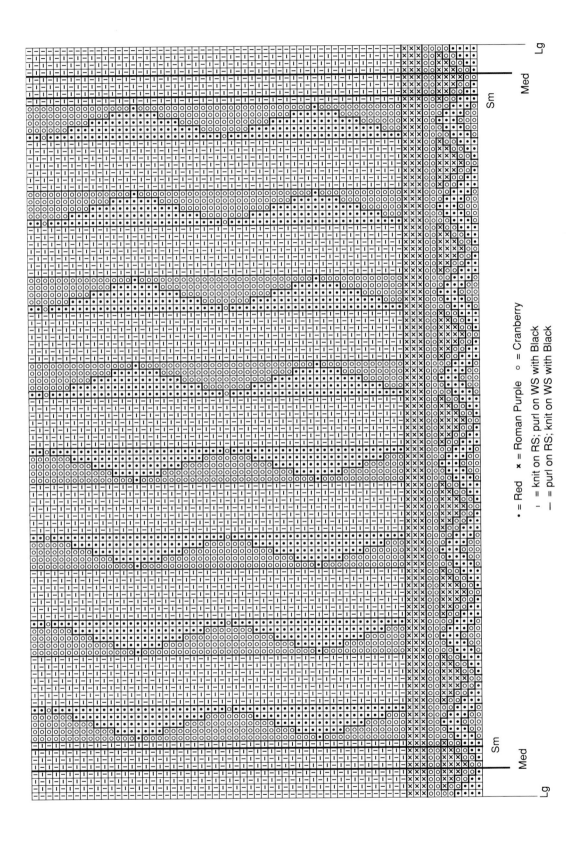

• = Red x = Roman Purple ○ = Cranberry

ı = knit on RS; purl on WS with Black
— = purl on RS; knit on WS with Black

53

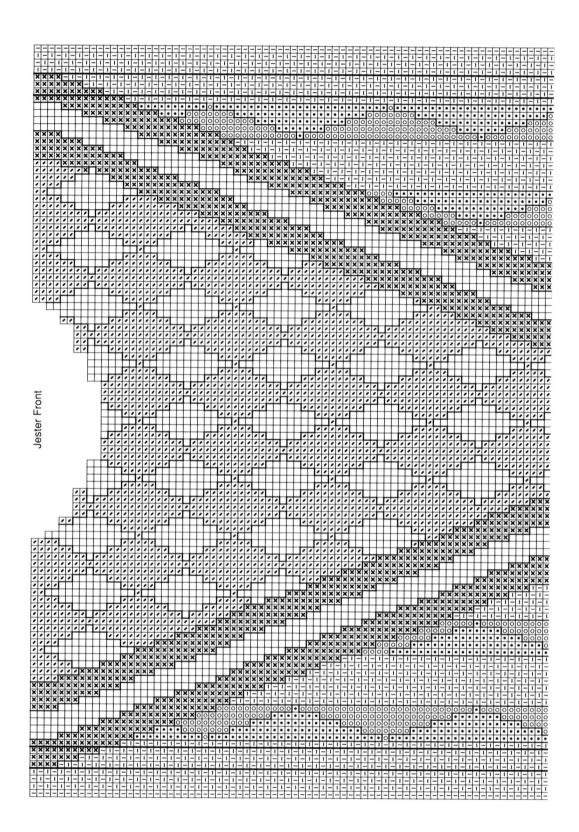

Jester Front

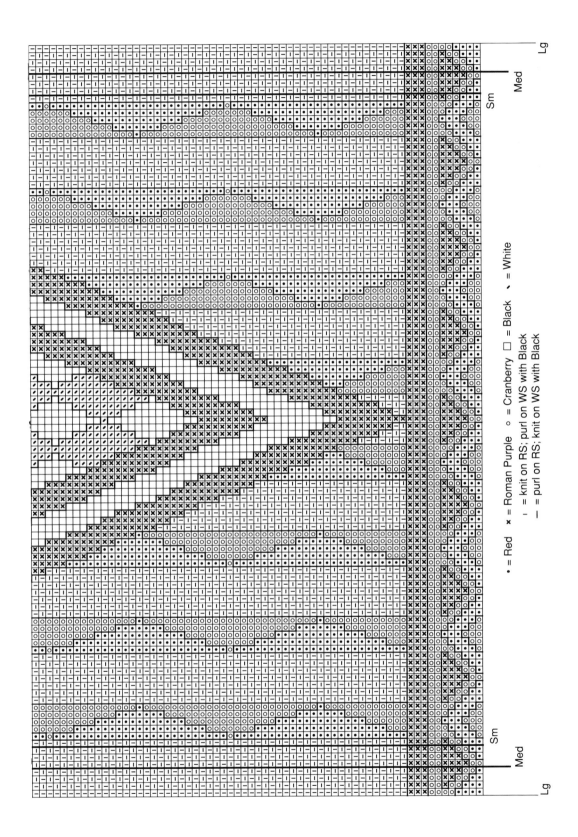

• = Red × = Roman Purple ○ = Cranberry □ = Black ﹨ = White

| = knit on RS; purl on WS with Black

— = purl on RS; knit on WS with Black

Lg

Med

Sm

Sm

Med

Lg

Rose and Vine
Body Lace Border

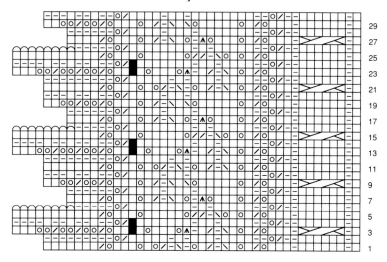

Rose and Vine
Sleeve Lace Border

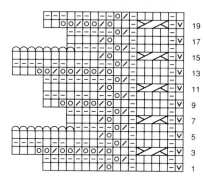

□ = knit on RS, purl on WS　　– = purl on RS, knit on WS　　∕ = k2tog　　＼ = ssk

o = yarn over　　▲ = slip 1 knitwise, k2tog, psso　　■ = no stitch　　v = slip st　　∩ = bind off

Body Lace Border

▷╳◁ = 3/3 RC

Place 3 sts on cn to back, k3, k3 on cn

Note: Cable pattern is 6 rows. Lace pattern is 10 rows. 30 rows must be worked for one complete multiple pattern repeat.

Set-up row: CO 41 sts.
Row 1: (RS) K1, p1, k6, p1, k3, yo, k2tog, k1, yo, k1, ssk, p1, k2tog, k1, yo, p1, ssk, p1, k2tog, [yo, k1] twice, k2, yo, k2tog, k7.
Row 2: K9, yo, k2tog, p5, k1, p1, k1, p3, k1, p4, k2, yo, k2tog, k2, p6, k1, p1.
Row 3: K1, p1, 3/3RC, p1, k3, yo, k2tog, k1, yo, k1, ssk, p1, k2tog, k1, p1, sl1 knitwise, k2tog, psso, [yo, k3] twice, yo, [k2tog, yo twice] 3 times, k3.
Row 4: K4, [p1, k2] 3 times, yo, k2tog, p7, k1, p2, k1, p4, k2, yo, k2tog, k2, p6, k1, p1.
Row 5: K1, p1, k6, p1, k3, yo, k2tog, [k1, yo] twice, ssk, p1, [k2tog] twice, yo, k5, yo, k3, yo, k2tog, k11.
Row 6: BO 7 sts, k5, yo, k2tog, p8, k1, p1, k1, p5, k2, yo, k2tog, k2, p6, k1, p1.
Row 7: K1, p1, k6, p1, k3, yo, k2tog, k1, yo, k3, yo, sl1 knitwise, k2tog, psso, p1, yo, k1, ssk, p1, k2tog, k1, yo, k3, yo, k2tog, k4.
Row 8: K6, yo, k2tog, p4, k1, p3, k1, p7, k2, yo, k2tog, k2, p6, k1, p1.
Row 9: K1, p1, 3/3RC, p1, k3, yo, k2tog, k1, yo, k5, yo, ssk, k1, ssk, p1, k2tog, k1, yo, k3, yo, [k2tog, yo twice] twice, k2.
Row 10: K3, [p1, k2] twice, yo, k2tog, p4, k1, p2, k1, p8, k2, yo, k2tog, k2, p6, k1, p1.
Following graph, work Rows 1-30 for 1 complete pattern repeat.

Sleeve Lace Border

▷╳◁ = 2/2 RC

Place 2 sts on cn to back, k2, k2 on cn

Note: Cable pattern is 4 rows. Lace pattern is 10 rows. 20 rows must be worked for one complete multiple pattern repeat.

Set-up row: CO 18 sts.
Row 1: K1, p1, k4, p1, k2, yo, k2tog, k7.
Row 2: K9, yo, k2tog, k1, p4, k1, p1.
Row 3: K1, p1, 2/2RC, p1, k2, yo, [k2tog, yo twice] 3 times, k3.
Row 4: K4, [p1, k2] 3 times, yo, k2tog, k1, p4, k1, p1.
Row 5: K1, p1, k4, p1, k2, yo, k2tog, k11.
Row 6: BO 7 sts, k5, yo, k2tog, k1, p4, k1, p1.
Row 7: K1, p1, 2/2RC, p1, k2, yo, k2tog, k4.
Row 8: K6, yo, k2tog, k1, p4, k1, p1.
Row 9: K1, p1, k4, p1, k2, yo, [k2tog, yo twice] twice, k2.
Row 10: K3, [p1, k2] twice, yo, k2tog, k1, p4, k1, p1.
Following graph, work Rows 1-20 for 1 complete pattern repeat.

Jewel Coat

Jewel Coat

Sizes Medium (Large)
Finished Chest Measurement:
52 (60)"
Full Length: 42 (46½)"
Sleeve Length: 17 (18½)"
Sleeve Width: 19½ (22)"

Charts: refer to pages 73–75

Materials
Mohair 90
(90% mohair, 6% polyester,
4% acrylic, 50gm skein =
approximately 115 yards)
9 skeins color A, Moody
Blue
3 skeins color B, Turkish Gem
1 skein color C, Indigo
Fashion
1 skein color D, Sapphire
3 skeins color E, Autumn
Russet
1 skein color F, Creme de
Menthe
1 skein color G, Jezabel
1 skein color H, Golden Sun
2 skeins color I, Velvet Port
1 skein color J, Ebony
1 skein color K, Crimson Lake
Impulse
(58% wool, 37% mohair, 5%
nylon, 50gm skein =
approximately 105 yards)
2 skeins color L, Atlantis
Body needle sizes under Gauge
Rib needle sizes 6 or 7
Bobbins

The changing of darkness into light and of light into color flows like the transformation of primitive rock into precious stone. For as light passes through

facets carefully cut and polished with time, its unpredictable journey is recorded by an ever changing kaleidoscope of color taking it from a daytime piece to a glittering nighttime setting.

Gauge
18 sts and 22 rows = 4" over
colorwork using size 9 needles
or size required to achieve
correct gauge.
16 sts and 20 rows = 4" over
colorwork using size 10
needles or size required to
achieve correct gauge.

Pattern Stitches
Stockinette Stitch
Row 1: (RS) Knit.
Row 2: Purl.
Seed Stitch
Row 1: (RS) *K1, p1; rep
from*.
All subsequent rows - Knit
the purls and purl the
knits.
Intarsia technique (see
Knitting Techniques) used
throughout.

Note
Work individual color
areas with separate bobbins of
color.

Back
With smaller needles and color
L, CO 107 sts. Work Seed st
for 2½". Change to larger
needles and color B. WS
facing, p1 row inc 13 sts
evenly spaced – 120 sts. Work

Back chart to beginning of neck shaping. **Shape neck:** RS facing, work 44 sts in established pattern. Place center 32 sts on hold. Join new yarns. Work 44 sts in established pattern. Working both sides at the same time, at each neck edge on every other row, BO 2 sts twice. Place rem 40 shoulder sts on hold.

Left Front

With smaller needles and color L, CO 67 sts. Work rib as for Back ending on RS row. Seed 13 sts and place on hold. Change to larger needles and color B. Purl rem sts. Work Left Front chart to beginning of neck shaping. **Shape neck:** WS facing, at neck edge BO 8 sts. On every other row, BO 3 sts twice, then 2 sts 3 times. Work to end of chart. Place rem 40 shoulder sts on hold.

Right Front

Work rib as for Left Front. Work Right Front chart reversing neck shaping.

Sleeves

With smaller needles and color L, CO 42 sts (both sizes). Work rib as for Back. Change to larger needles. Work Sleeve chart, inc 1 st each end every other row once, every 4 rows 3 times, [every other row, every 4 rows] twice, every 4 rows once, other other row once, every 4 rows twice, every other row once, every 4 rows 3 times, [every other row once, every 4 rows twice] twice, every 4 rows once – 88 sts. Work to end of chart or desired length. BO loosely.

Left Front Border

Slip 13 sts on hold to smaller needles. Work Seed st for same length as front. Place sts on hold. Sew border to Left Front.

Right Front Border

Work as for Left Front border.

Neck band

Knit shoulder seams of Front and Back tog (see Knitting Techniques). With smaller needles, color L and RS facing, work Seed st across 13 sts on right front border, pick up and k17 sts along neck edge, 6 sts along back neck, 32 sts on hold, 6 sts along back neck, 18 sts along neck edge, and 13 sts on hold – 105 sts. Work Seed st for 2½". BO loosely in pattern.

Finishing

Measure down 10 (11)" from shoulder seam on Front and Back. Mark for underarm. Set in sleeves between markers. Sew side and sleeve seams matching patterns.

Aztec Jazz

Aztec Jazz

Sizes Small /Medium
(Medium/Large)
Finished Chest measurement:
44 (48)"
Full Length: 28½"
Sleeve Length: 20"
Sleeve Width: 21 (22½)"

Charts: refer to pages 76–77

Materials
Luxury Crepe
(100% wool, 50gm skein
= approximately 107 yds)
1 skein color A, Chartreuse
3 skeins color B, Forest
2 skeins color C, Kingfisher
2 skeins color D, Rust
2 skeins color E, Cardinal
1 skein color F, New York
8 skeins color G, Stone
Needle sizes 5 and 6 or
size required to achieve
correct gauge.
Size 6, 24" circular needle
Bobbins

Gauge
22 sts and 28 rows = 4" over
colorwork using larger needles

Pattern Stitches
1x1 Corrugated Rib
Row 1: (RS) *K1C, p1B; rep
from*, end k1C.
Row 2: *P1C, k1B, rep from*,
end p1C.

*Inspiration comes
from an
extemporaneous
musical medium called
jazz. Like jazz, this
pattern selection of
native Mexican art
relies on individual
and collective
improvisations of basic
colors, shapes, and*

*patterns to successfully
create rhythmic
variations of a classic
theme. Colorful
symbolic references
and dramatic,
decorative touches
transcend tradition to
offer a lively addition
to any casual occasion.*

Stockinette Stitch
Row 1: (RS) Knit.
Row 2: Purl.
Intarsia technique (see Knitting
Techniques) used throughout
body of sweater.
Fair isle technique (see Knitting
Techniques) is used in a
portion of the neck band.

Note
Work individual color
blocks with separate
bobbins of color.

Back
With smaller needles and
color C, CO 121 (133)
sts. Work 1x1 Corrugated
rib for 2". Change to
larger needles. Work Back
chart to beginning of neck
shaping. **Shape neck:**
RS facing, work 52 (58)
sts in established pattern.
Place center 17 sts on
hold. Join new yarns.
Work 52 (58) sts in established
pattern. Working both sides at
the same time, at each neck
edge on every other row, BO 5
sts twice, 3 sts twice, 2 sts
once, 3 sts twice, 2 sts 6
times, [1 st once, 2 sts once]
twice, 1 st twice, and 2 sts
once. Work to end of chart.
Place rem 6 (12) sts on hold.

Aztec Jazz

Front

Work as for Back to front neck shaping. **Shape neck:** RS facing, work 60 (66) sts in established pattern. BO center st. Join new yarns. Work 60 (66) sts in established pattern. Working both sides at the same time, at each neck edge on every other row, dec 1 st 54 times. Work to end of chart. Place rem 6 (12) shoulder sts on hold.

Sleeves

With smaller needles and color C, CO 49 (57) sts. Join color B. Work rib as for Back. Change to larger needles. Work Sleeve chart, inc 1 st each end [every 4 rows twice, every other row once] 7 times, then every 4 rows 13 times – 117 (125) sts. Work to end of chart or desired length. BO loosely.

Neck band

Knit shoulder sts of Front and Back tog (see Knitting Techniques). With circular needle, color G, and RS facing, beginning at center front, pick up and knit 93 sts along right front neck edge, 50 sts along right back neck edge, 17 center back sts on hold, 50 sts along left back neck edge, and 92 sts along left front neck edge – 302 sts. Do not join. Turn, k1 row. Join colors as indicated and work Rows 1-10 of neck chart in *fair isle technique* and Rows 11-28 in *intarsia technique.* Work 5 rows of 1x1 Corrugated rib as for Back. Work 2 rows reverse St st. BO loosely in purl.

Finishing

Sew right side of neck band over left side along pick-up edge. Measure down $10\frac{1}{2}$ ($11\frac{1}{4}$)" from shoulder seam on Front and Back. Mark for underarm. Set in sleeves between markers. Sew side and sleeve seams.

Alternate color choice for garment: Porcelain, Navy, Honesty, Kingfisher, Raspberry, Mill Pond.

Neck Border

□ = New York
■ = Forest
○ = Rust
● = Cardinal
× = Kingfisher
✳ = Chartreuse
□ = Stone

Repeat | Begin

Indian Summer

Indian Summer

Size Medium/Large
Finished Chest Measurement:
51"
Full Length: 32"
Sleeve Length: 19½"
Sleeve Width: 22½"

Charts: refer to pages 78–82

Materials
Kiwi Splendour
(100% wool, 100gm skein
= approximately 111 yds)
Alternate yarn choice
Optimum Performance
(100% wool, 100gm skein
= 144 yds)
4 skeins color A, Tawny Red
3 skeins color B, Maroon
6 skeins color C, Dark Brown
2 skeins color D, Donegal
2 skeins color E, Gold
1 skein color F, Peacock
1 skein color G, Navy
Needle sizes 7 and 9 or
size required to achieve
correct gauge.
Bobbins
Ten ½" buttons

Gauge
16 sts and 20 rows = 4" over
colorwork using larger needles

The warmth of those fleeting days before summer turns to fall is successfully captured in this colorful attempt to make Indian Summer last forever. Graphically

detailed with splashes of gold, this generous sweater coat encourages long walks along country lanes with its comfortable style and casual spirit.

Pattern Stitches
Seeded rib
Row 1: *K1, p1; rep from*.
Row 2: *P2, k1; rep from*.
(See note.)
Stockinette Stitch
Row 1: (RS) Knit.
Row 2: Purl.
Intarsia technique (see Knitting
Techniques) used throughout.

Note
The Seeded rib (see chart
on page 66) gives you
'knit, purl, knit' vertical
columns with 3 seed
stitches in between each
column.

Back
With smaller needles and
color C, CO 102 sts.
Work Seeded rib for 3".
Change to larger needles.
Work Back chart to
beginning of neck
shaping. **Shape neck:** RS
facing, work 30 sts in
established pattern. Place
center 42 sts on hold. Join new
yarns. Work 30 sts in
established pattern. Working
both sides at the same time, at
each neck edge on every other
row, BO 1 st twice. Work to
end of chart. Place rem 28
shoulder sts on hold.

Indian Summer

Left Front

With smaller needles and color C, CO 60 sts. Work rib as for Back. Change to larger needles. Work 33 sts of Left Front chart. Place rem 27 sts on hold (front border). Work Left Front chart to beginning of neck shaping, inc 1 st on row 55. **Shape neck**: WS facing, dec 1 st on next, then every 8 rows 6 times. Work to end of chart. Place rem 28 shoulder sts on hold.

Right Front

Work rib as for Left Front for 8 rows. **Buttonhole row**: Rib 4 sts (k2tog, yo); rib 16 sts (k2tog, yo); rib to end of row. Continue in Seeded rib for 3", ending 27 sts before end of last row. Place rem sts on hold. Change to larger needles. Work Right Front chart reversing neck shaping.

Sleeves

With smaller needles and color C, CO 45 sts. Work rib as for Back, inc 2 sts on last row of rib. Change to larger needles. Work Sleeve chart, inc 1 st each end every 4 rows 21 times – 89 sts. Work to end of chart or desired length. BO loosely.

Left Front Border and Collar

Knit shoulder sts of Front and Back tog (see Knitting Techniques). Place 27 sts on hold onto smaller needles. Work even in Seeded rib to beginning of neck shaping. Inc 1 st on inside edge of collar every 8 rows, 8 times – 35 sts. Work even in Seeded rib to center Back. End on WS row. Place sts on spare double pointed needle.

Right Front Border and Collar

Place 27 sts on hold onto smaller needles. Work even in Seeded rib to beginning of neck shaping, and *at the same time*, work buttonholes as before every 24 rows, 4 more times. **Shape Collar:** Inc 1 st on inside edge of collar every 8 rows, 8 times – 35 sts. Work even in Seeded rib to center Back. End on RS row. With RS of collar facing, knit sts tog from outside edge to inside edge.

Finishing

Sew Front Borders to front edging and shaped edge of collar to neck edge. Measure down 11½" from shoulder seam on Front and Back. Mark for underarm. Set in sleeves between markers. Sew side and sleeve seams matching patterns. Sew on buttons.

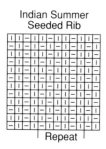

Indian Summer
Seeded Rib

Repeat

ı = knit on RS; purl on WS

– = purl on RS; knit on WS

Stained Glass

The stained glass windows of St. Paul's Cathedral in London were the inspiration for this design. The designer, moved by

their depth and fluidness as the sun gave them life, created this impressionistic treatment of the language of light.

Sizes Small (Medium, Large)
Finished Chest Measurement:
45 (49, 53)"
Full Length: 27"
Sleeve Length: 18½"
Sleeve Width: 22"

Charts: refer to pages 83–88

Materials
Crucci Baby Soft Mohair
(80% Mohair, 18% wool, 2% nylon, 50gm skein = approximately 109 yds)
2 skeins color A, Ocean
3 skeins color B, Currant
1 skein color C, Sunflower
2 skeins color D, Wilderness
1 skein color E, Cardinal
3 skeins color F, Midnight
1 skein color G, Khaki
1 skein color H, Peacock
Needle sizes 8 and 10 or size required to achieve correct gauge.
Bobbins
Seven ½" buttons

Gauge
16 sts and 20 rows = 4" over colorwork using larger needles

Pattern Stitches
1x1 Rib
Row 1: (RS) *K1, p1; rep from*.
Row 2: Knit the knits and purl the purls.
Stockinette Stitch
Row 1: (RS) Knit.
Row 2: Purl.
Intarsia technique (see Knitting Techniques) used throughout.

Note
Work individual color blocks with separate bobbins of color.

Back
With smaller needles and color B, CO 90 (98, 106) sts. Work 1x1 Rib for 2". Change to larger needles. Work Back chart to beginning of neck shaping. **Shape neck:** RS facing, work 35 (39, 43) sts in established pattern. Place center 20 sts on hold. Join new yarns. Work 35 (39, 43) sts in established pattern. Working both sides at the same time, at each neck edge on every other row, BO 4 sts once, 3 sts once. Work to end of chart. Place rem 28 (32, 36) shoulder sts on hold.

Left Front

With smaller needles and color B, CO 41 (45, 49) sts. Work rib as for Back. Change to larger needles. Work Left Front chart to beginning of neck shaping. **Shape neck:** WS facing, BO 2 sts. At neck edge, on every other row, BO 3 sts once, 2 sts 3 times, then 1 st twice. Work to end of chart. Place rem 28 (32, 36) shoulder sts on hold.

Right Front

Work rib as for Left Front. Work Right Front chart reversing neck shaping.

Left Sleeve

With smaller needles and color B, CO 44 sts (all sizes). Work rib as for Back, inc 4 sts evenly spaced on last row – 48 sts. Change to larger needles. Work Left Sleeve chart, inc 1 st each end every 4 rows 19 times, then every other row once – 88 sts. Work to end of chart or desired length. BO loosely.

Right Sleeve

Work rib as for Left Sleeve, inc 4 sts evenly spaced on last row – 48 sts. Change to larger needles. Work Right Sleeve chart, working incs as for Left Sleeve. Work to end of chart or desired length. BO loosely.

Left Front Button Band

With smaller needles and color B, CO 12 sts. Work 1x1 Rib for 127 rows. Place sts on hold. Sew band to left front.

Right Front Buttonhole Band

With smaller needles and color B, CO 12 sts. Work 1x1 Rib for 4 rows. **Buttonhole row:** Rib 4 sts, yo, k2tog, rib to end of row. *Work 21 rows in rib and rep buttonhole; rep from* 4 more times. Continue in rib for 127 rows total. Place sts on hold. Sew band to right front.

Neck band

Knit shoulder sts of Front and Back tog (see Knitting Techniques). With smaller needles, color B, and RS facing, work 1x1 Rib across 12 sts on right front band, pick up and k71 sts along neck edge, work rib across rem 12 sts on hold – 95 sts. Work rib for 4 rows. On row 5 of right front neck band, make last buttonhole as previously worked. Work rib for 8 more rows. Make buttonhole. Work rib for 4 more rows. BO loosely in rib. Fold neck band to inside and sew in place.

Finishing

Measure down 11" (all sizes) from shoulder seam on Front and Back. Mark for underarm. Set in sleeves between markers. Sew side and sleeve seams matching patterns. Sew on buttons.

Alternate color choice for garment: Wilderness, Cyclamen, Whisper, Fuchsia, Melon, Lavender, Peacock, Cardinal.

Rose and Vine

Rose and Vine

Sizes Small (Medium, Large)
Finished Body Measurement:
42 (46, 50)"
Full Length: 28½"
Sleeve Length: 17½ (18½, 18½)"
Sleeve Width: 20 (21, 22)"

Charts: refer to page 56

Materials
Eagle USA Glen Mist
(100% wool, 50gm skein =
approximately 133 yds)
21 skeins A, Wild Iris
Embroidery Colors
1 skein color B, Bottle
1 skein color C, Burgundy
1 skein color D, Iris
1 skein color E, Mallow
1 skein color F, Soft Pink
Needle sizes 5 and 6 or
size required to achieve
correct gauge.
Size 7, 16" circular needle
Cable needle

Gauge
24 sts and 32 rows = 4"
over St st using larger needles

Pattern Stitches
Panel A
Row 1: (RS) K32 (39, 44),
p1, sl1, p1, k14, p1, sl1, p1.
Row 2: K1, p1, k1, p14, k1,
p1, k1, p39.
Panel B
C3F
Place 2 sts on cn to front, k1,
k2 on cn.

The elegant, flowing lines of this sweater were inspired by the beauty of a single bud as its delicate petals gently unfolded in the warmth of a morning sun. Heavily embroidered with traveling vines and

leaves, it represents an allusion to quieter times past, of politeness, parasols and gentleness of spirit. The intricate detail of a decorative lattice border adds definition like the ornamental fence of an English country garden.

C3B
Place 1 st on cn to back, k2,
k1 on cn.
2/2RC
Place 2 sts on cn to back, k2,
k2 on cn.
Row 1: K1, C3F, k14, C3B, k1.
Row 2 and all WS rows: P22.
Row 3: K2, C3F, k12, C3B, k2.
Row 5: K3, C3F, k10, C3B, k3.
Row 7: K4, C3F, k8, C3B, k4.
Row 9: K5, C3F, k6, C3B, k5.
Row 11: K6, C3F, k4, C3B, k6.
Row 13: K7, C3F, k2, C3B, k7.
Row 15: K8, C3F, C3B, k8.
Rows 17 & 21: K9, 2/2RC, k9.
Row 19: K 22.
Row 23: K8, C3B, C3F, k8.
Row 25: K7, C3B, k2, C3F, k7.
Row 27: K6, C3B, k4, C3F, k6.
Row 29: K5, C3B, k6, C3F, k5.
Row 31: K4, C3B, k8, C3F, k4.
Row 33: K3, C3B, k10, C3F, k3.
Row 35: K2, C3B, k12, C3F, k2.
Row 37: K1, C3B, k14, C3F, k1.
Row 39: C3B, k16, C3F.
Row 41: C3F, k16, C3B.
Panel C
Row 1: (RS) P1, sl1, p1, k14,
p1, sl1, p1, k32 (39, 44).
Row 2: P39, k1, p1, k1, p14,
k1, p1, k1.

Rose and Vine

Double Seed
Row 1: *K2, p2; rep from*.
Rows 2 & 4: Knit the knits and purl the purls.
Row 3: *P2, k2; rep from*.
Stockinette Stitch
Row 1: (RS) Knit.
Row 2: Purl.

Back

With smaller needles and color A, CO 41 sts. Work Body Lace border pattern (chart and instructions on page 56) for 21 (23, 25)". BO loosely. Change to larger needles. With WS facing, pick up 126 (140, 150) sts along cable edge. Work St st for 179 rows. **Shape neck:** WS facing, work 46 (53, 58) sts in pattern. Place center 34 sts on hold. Join new yarn. Work 46 (53, 58) sts in pattern. Working both sides at the same time, at each neck edge on every other row, BO 2 sts twice. Place rem 42 (49, 54) shoulder sts on hold.

Front

Work Lace border as for Back. BO loosely. Change to larger needles. With WS facing, pick up 127 (141, 151) sts along cable edge. Work St st for 18 rows. WS facing, (p2tog, yo) 63 (70, 75) times, end p1. Next row: (k2tog, yo) 63 (70, 75) times, end k1. Purl across

and dec 1 st – 126 (140, 150) sts. Work 52 (59, 64) sts of Panel A, 22 sts of Panel B, 52 (59, 64) sts of Panel C. Rep Rows 1-42 of panel B 3 times. **Shape neck:** WS facing, work 48 (55, 60) sts in pattern. Place center 30 sts on hold. Join new yarn. Work 48 (55, 60) sts in pattern. Working both sides at the same time, at each neck edge on every other row, BO 2 sts 3 times. Place rem 42 (49, 54) shoulder sts on hold.

Sleeves

With smaller needles and color A, CO 18 sts. Work Sleeve Lace border pattern (chart and instructions on page 56) for 9". BO loosely. Change to larger needles. With WS facing, pick up 60 (64, 68) sts along cable edge. Work 1 row St st. Work Double seed pattern inc 1 st each end every 4 rows 30 (31, 32) times –120 (126, 132) sts. Work St st for 2" (Rosebud and Vine sleeve border). BO loosely.

Neck band

Knit shoulder sts of Front and Back tog. With circular needle, color A, and starting at left shoulder, pick up 12 sts along left neck edge, 30 sts on hold at center front, 12 sts along right neck edge, 6 sts along

right back neck, 34 sts on hold at center back, 6 sts along left back neck – 100 sts. Join and knit 11 rows. Next row (picot edge) *k2tog, yo; rep from*. Work 1x1 rib for 10 rows. BO loosely.

Notes

Following chart, duplicate stitch roses for front, sleeve border, and neck band before finishing. Embroider vines in back stitch and leaves in satin stitch using photograph as a guide.

Finishing

Fold neck band to inside. Slip st in place. Measure down 10 (11, 12)" from shoulder seam on Front and Back. Mark for underarm. Set in sleeves between markers. Sew side and sleeve seams.

Rose and Vine
Duplicate Stitch Chart

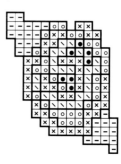

× = Burgundy o = Iris ⟍ = Mallow

− = Bottle • = Soft Pink

Using photograph as a guide, rotate chart for placement of roses and leaves on sweater.

Jewel Sleeve

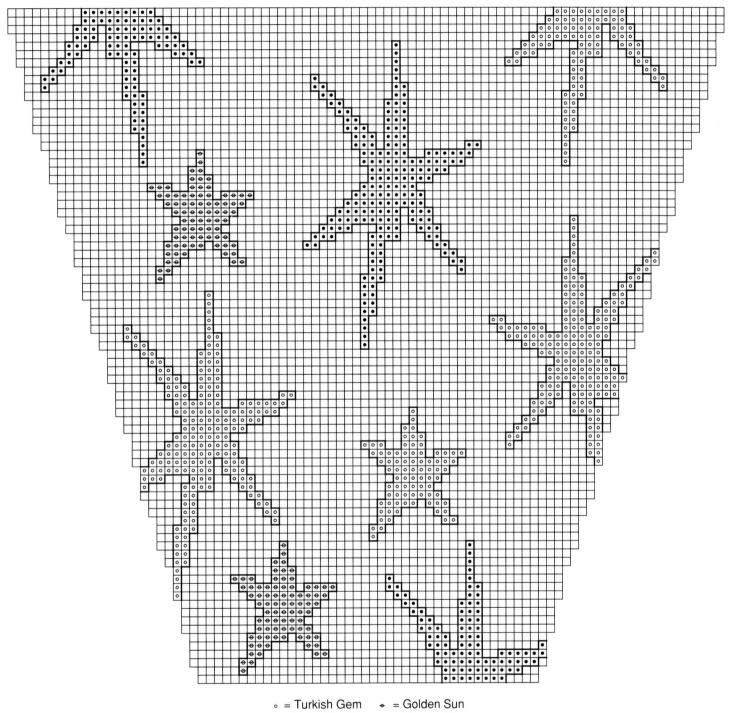

○ = Turkish Gem   ⊕ = Golden Sun
● = Velvet Port   □ = Moody Blue

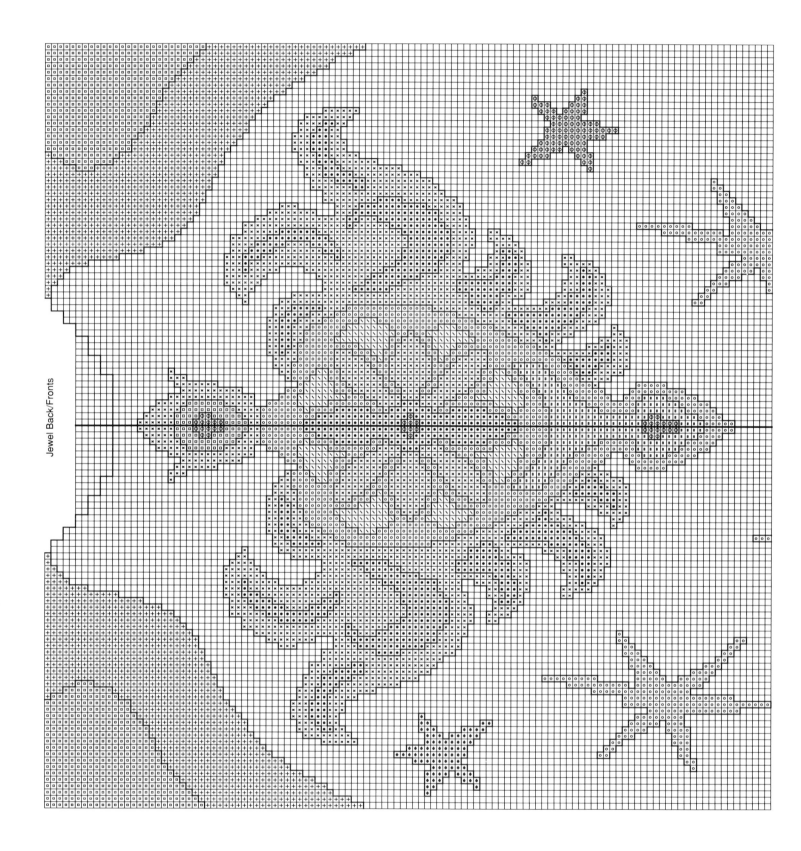

Jewel Back/Fronts

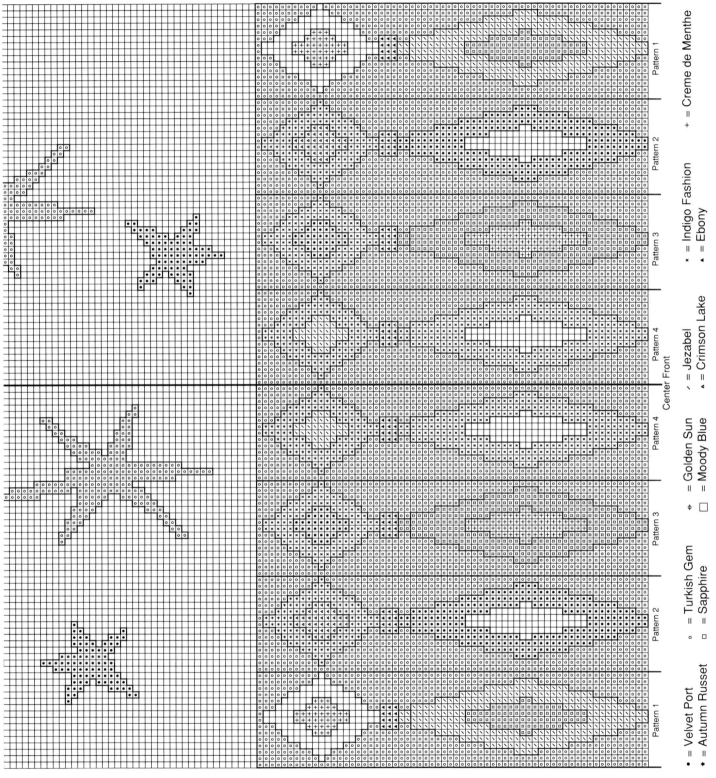

Pattern 1

Pattern 2

Pattern 3

Pattern 4

Center Front

Pattern 4

Pattern 3

Pattern 2

Pattern 1

• = Velvet Port   ○ = Turkish Gem   ◆ = Golden Sun   ✓ = Jezabel   × = Indigo Fashion   + = Creme de Menthe

✶ = Autumn Russet   □ = Sapphire   ☐ = Moody Blue   ◢ = Crimson Lake   ◂ = Ebony

Back: Work Patterns 4, 1, 2, 3, then 1, 2, 3, 4 for bottom border. This prevents repetition of bottom patterns at side seams. Work Fronts as shown.

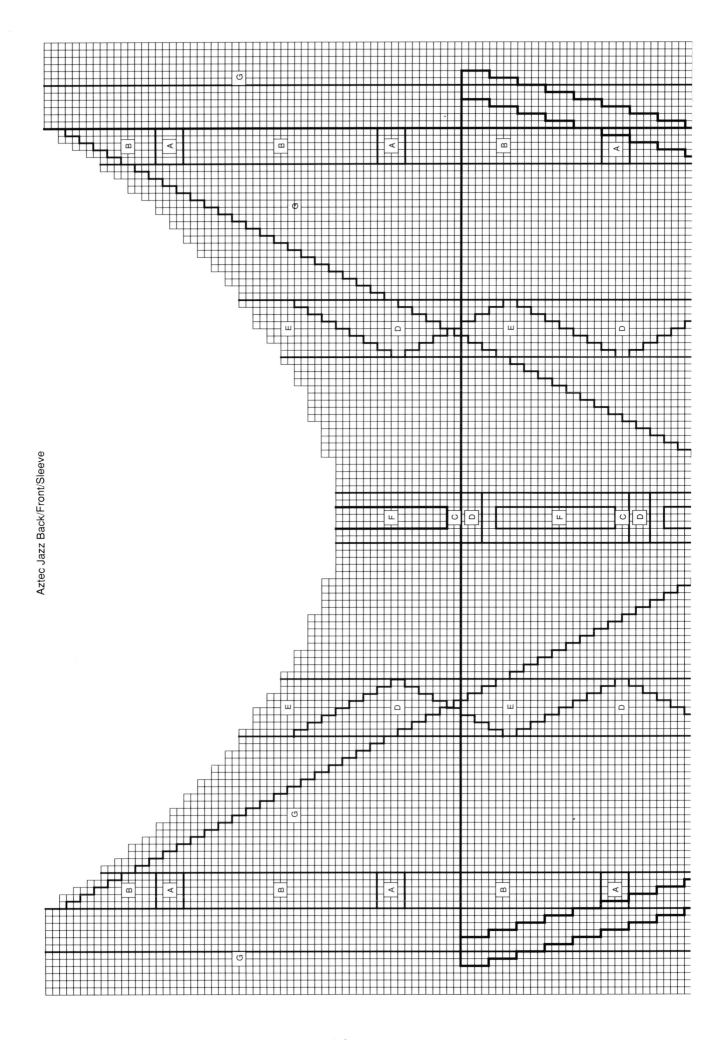

Aztec Jazz Back/Front/Sleeve

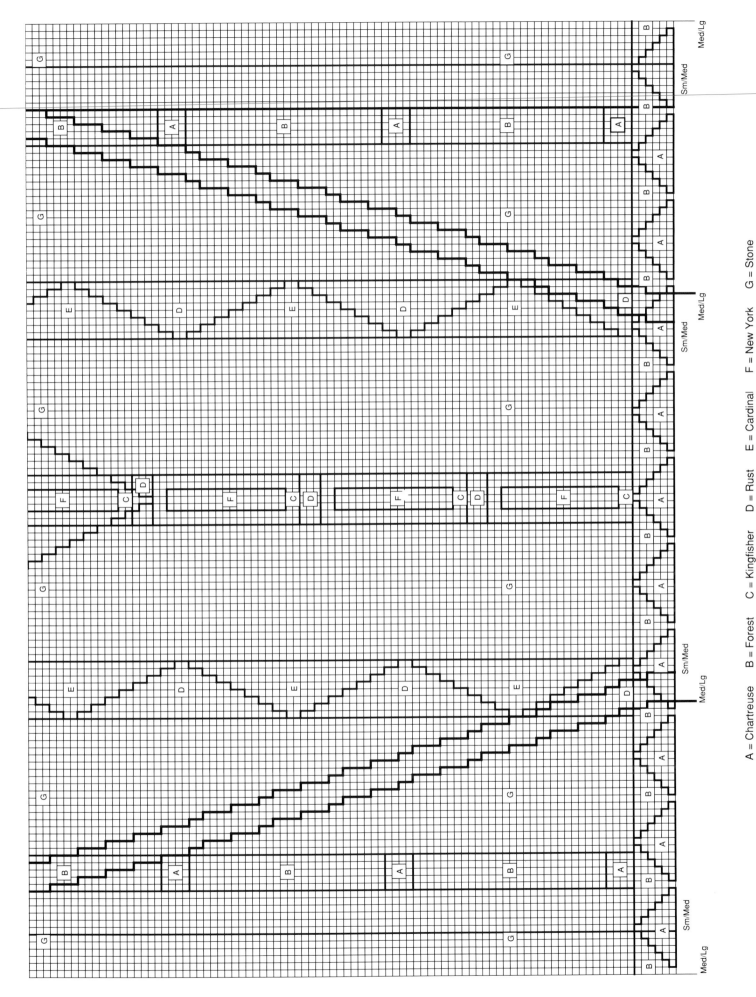

A = Chartreuse   B = Forest   C = Kingfisher   D = Rust   E = Cardinal   F = New York   G = Stone

77

Indian Summer Back

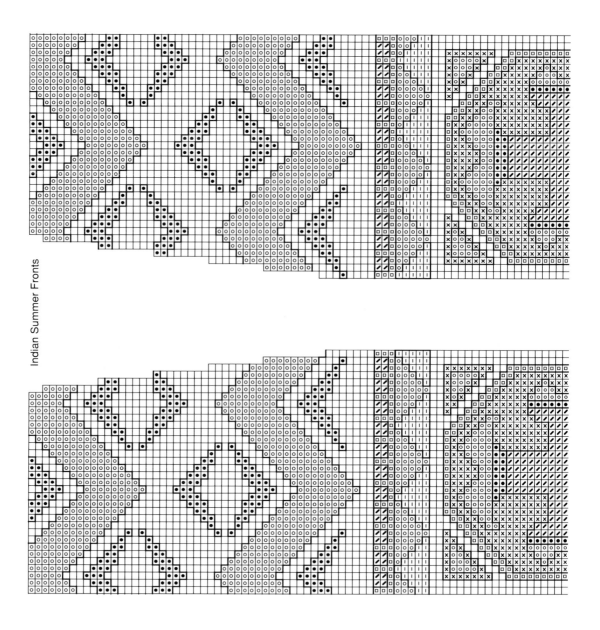

Indian Summer Fronts

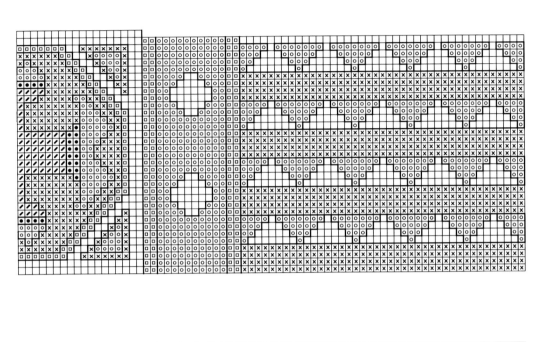

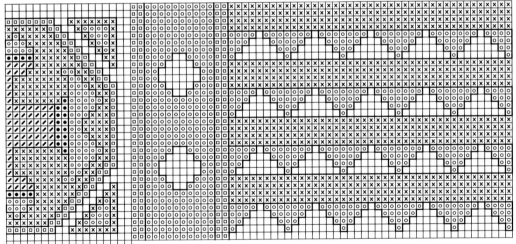

□ = Peacock   o = Maroon   ● = Gold   ✔ = Navy   x = Donegal   ‑ = Dark Brown   ▢ = Tawny Red

Indian Summer Sleeve

□ = Peacock   ○ = Maroon   • = Gold   ＼ = Navy   × = Donegal   ☐ = Tawny Red

Stained Glass Right Sleeve

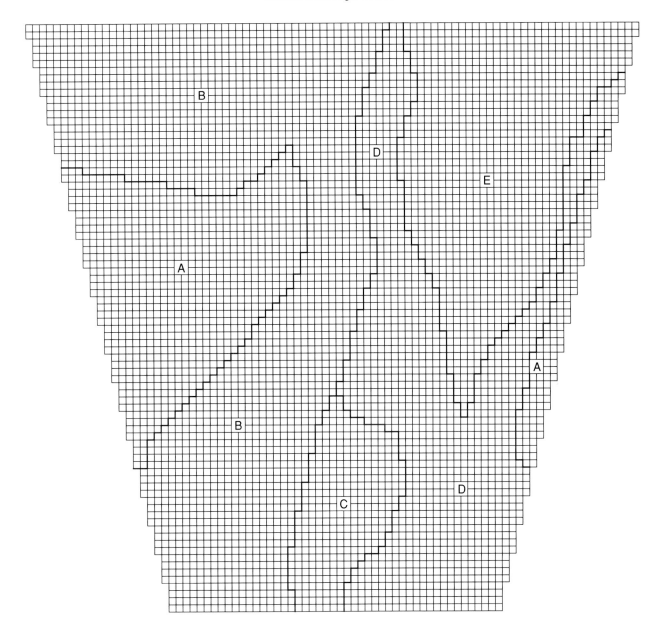

A = Ocean   B = Currant   C = Sunflower   D = Wilderness   E = Cardinal

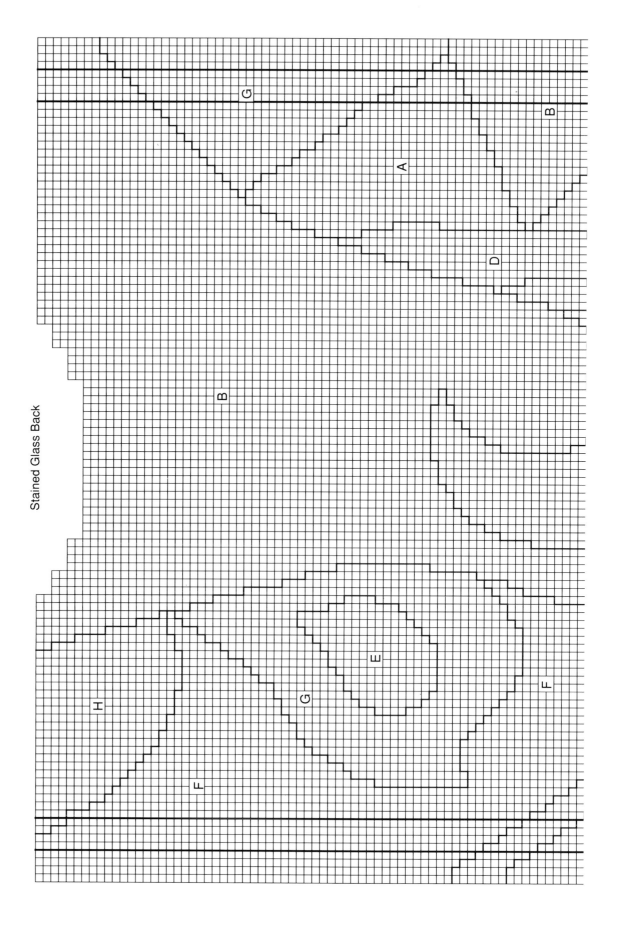

Stained Glass Back

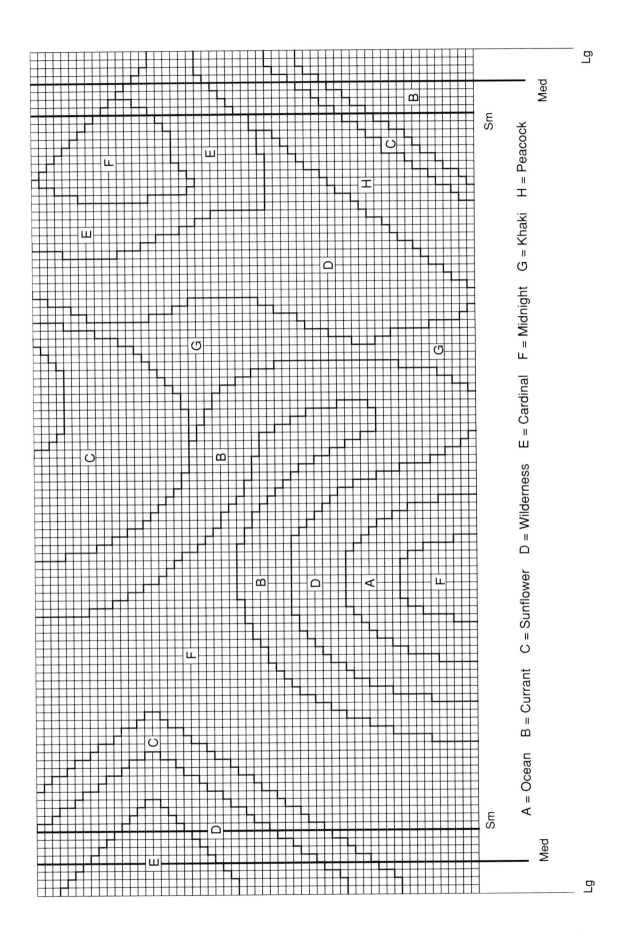

A = Ocean   B = Currant   C = Sunflower   D = Wilderness   E = Cardinal   F = Midnight   G = Khaki   H = Peacock

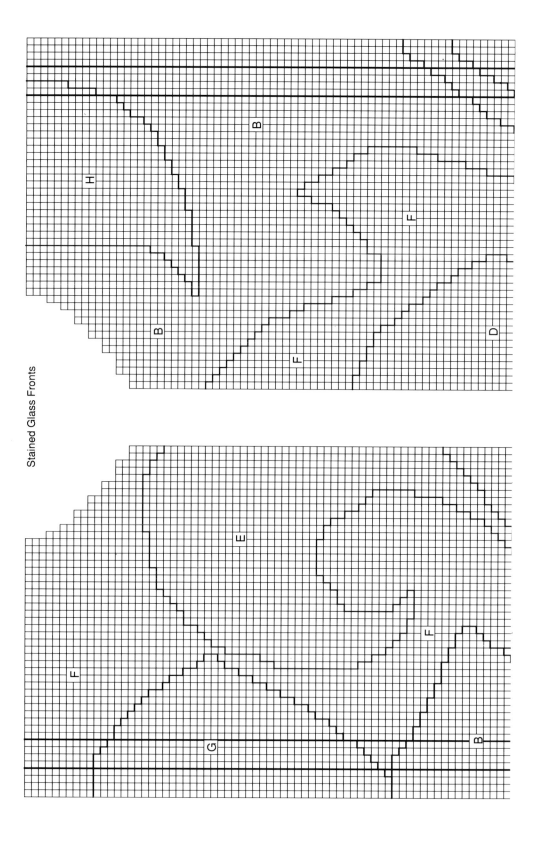

Stained Glass Fronts

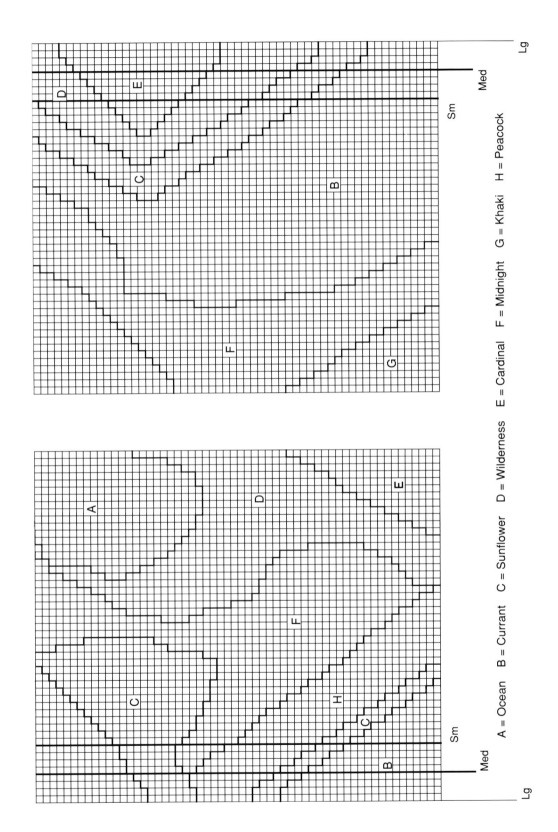

A = Ocean   B = Currant   C = Sunflower   D = Wilderness   E = Cardinal   F = Midnight   G = Khaki   H = Peacock

87

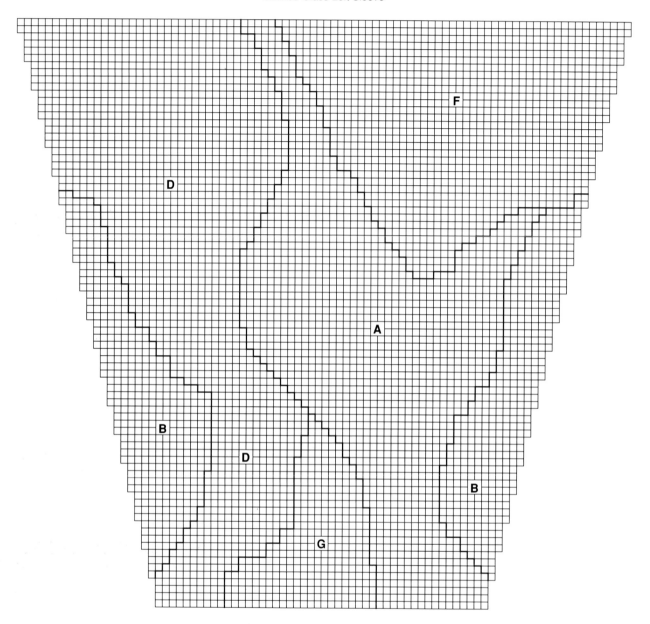

A = Ocean   B = Currant   D = Wilderness   F = Midnight   G = Khaki

Lotus Trellis

Lotus Trellis

Sizes Medium (Large)
Finished Chest Measurement: 54 (60)"
Full Length: 45 (49½)"
Sleeve Length: 16¾ (18¼)"
Sleeve Width: 19½ (22)"

Charts: refer to pages 105–109

Materials
Mohair 90
(90% mohair, 6% polyester, 4% acrylic, 50gm skein = approximately 115 yds)
10 skeins color A, Sapphire
2 skeins color B, Turkish Gem
1 skein color C, Jezabel
1 skein color D, Creme de Menthe
1 skein color E, Deep Pool
1 skein color F, Golden Sun
1 skein color G, Flaming June
1 skein color H, Velvet Port
Crucci Baby Soft Mohair
(80% Mohair, 18% wool; 2% nylon, 50gm skein = approximately 109 yds)
1 skein color I, Wilderness
Impulse
(58% wool, 37% mohair, 5% nylon, 50gm skein = approximately 105 yds)
4 skeins color J, Senator
3 skeins color K, Indigo
3 skeins color L, Atlantis
Body needle sizes under Gauge
Rib needle sizes 6 or 7
Bobbins
Beads & Feathers.

This magnificent coat was designed to capture the fun and excitement of an evening out with the glittering inspiration from the splash of neon lights, theatrical backdrops and the sumptuous luxury of

leathery limousines. Classic, fluid, flowing and totally forgiving, its regal coloring and daring ornamentation create a dramatic distance of elegance, mystery and intrigue to turn the most mundane occasion into a total event.

Gauge
18 sts and 22 rows = 4" over colorwork using size 8 needles or size required to achieve correct gauge.
16 sts and 20 rows = 4" over colorwork using size 9 needles or size required to achieve correct gauge.

Pattern Stitches
Stockinette Stitch
Row 1: (RS) Knit.
Row 2: Purl.
Garter Stitch
Knit every row.
Reverse Stockinette Stitch
Row 1: (RS) Purl.
Row 2: Knit.
Bobble Border (11 st blocks)
CO 11 sts.
Rows 1-9: With main block color J or K, knit (Garter st).
Row 10: With MC, k5; with contrast color J or K, [k, p, k, p, k] in next stitch. [Turn, k5 sts] 4 times. Turn, [k2 tog] twice, k1. Turn, sl1, k2 tog, psso; with MC, k5.
Rows 11-19: With MC, knit (Garter st).
Trellis Stitch (Multiple of 6+5)
Row 1: (RS) With color L, k1, p3, *with yarn in front, sl3 purlwise, p3; rep from* end k1.
Row 2: P1, k3, *with yarn in back, sl3 purlwise, k3; rep from* end p1.
Row 3: K1, p3, *k3, p3; rep from* end k1.

Lotus Trellis

Row 4: P1, k3, *p3, k3; rep from* end p1.

Row 5: K5, *insert point of right-hand needle upwards under the 2 strands in front of the sl sts and knit them tog with the next st (pull up loop), k5; rep from* to end.

Row 6: Rep Row 3.

Row 7: P1, *yarn forward, sl3 purlwise, p3; rep from* end p1.

Row 8: K1, *yarn back, sl3 purlwise, k3; rep from* end k1.

Row 9: Rep Row 4.

Row 10: Rep Row 3.

Row 11: K2, *pull up loop, k5; rep from* to last 3 sts, pull up loop, k2.

Row 12: Rep Row 4.

Intarsia technique (see Knitting Techniques) used throughout.

Back

With smaller needles and *color K, CO 11 sts, with color J, CO 11 sts; rep from* 5 times, end with color K, CO 11 sts – 143 sts. Work Bobble border over 19 rows. Cut K. WS facing, and color J, knit and dec 12 sts evenly spaced across row. Work 5 rows Rev St st, dec 5 sts evenly spaced on 3rd row – 126 sts. Join color A. Work St st for 4 rows. Join color J. RS facing, k1 row. Work Rev St st for 5 rows, dec 6 sts evenly spaced on 3rd row – 120 sts. Change to larger needles. Work Back chart to beginning of Trellis st. Work 59 sts, p2tog, work 59 sts – 119 sts. Next row: Work 54 sts, drop color A. Join color L. Work Row 1 of Trellis st. Drop color L.

Join color A, work to end. Follow chart working sts as indicated by symbols. Every 6 rows, loosely strand color L across next st group, so yarn will then be in position for next pattern row. Work to end of chart. Place all sts on hold.

Left Front

With smaller needles and *color J, CO 11 sts, with color K, CO 11 sts; rep from* twice, end with color J, CO 11 sts – 77 sts. Work Bobble border as for Back. WS facing, place first 11 sts on hold – 66 sts. Join color J. Knit and dec 5 sts evenly spaced across row – 61 sts. Work 5 rows Rev St st, dec 3 sts evenly spaced on 3rd row – 58 sts. Join color A. Work St st for 4 rows. Join color J. RS facing, k1 row. Work Rev St st for 5 rows, dec 3 sts evenly spaced on 3rd row – 55 sts. Change to larger needles. Work Left Front chart to beginning of neck shaping. **Shape neck**: WS facing, dec 1 st at neck edge. Dec 1 st [every 4 rows, then every 6 rows] 4 times, then every 4 rows 6 times. Work to end of chart. Place rem 40 shoulder sts on hold.

Right Front

Work border as for Left Front. Work Right Front chart reversing neck shaping.

Sleeves

With smaller needle and *color J, CO 11 sts, with color K, CO 11 sts; rep from* once – 44 sts. Work Bobble border as for Back. Change to larger needles. Work Sleeve chart, inc 1 st each end [every 4 rows, every 2 rows, then every 4 rows] 7 times, then every 4 rows once – 88 sts. Work to end of chart or desired length. BO loosely.

Left Front Border

Sl 11 sts to smaller needles. Join color K. *Work 19 rows of Bobble border. Change to color J. Rep from*. Alternating blocks of color, work 21 blocks. Place sts on hold.

Right Front Border

Work 20 blocks as for Left Front Border. Knit last blocks of right and left fronts tog at back of neck.

Trellis Piping

With smaller double pointed needles and color L, CO 7 sts. K1 row. At end of each row, slide sts to right end of needle and continue in St st. A tube will form. Work in this manner until tube is long enough to edge entire Trellis pattern.

Finishing

Knit shoulder sts of Front and Back tog (see Knitting Techniques). Sew Front borders and neck band in place. Measure $9^{3}/_{4}$ (11)" down from shoulder seam on Front and Back. Mark for underarm. Set in sleeves between markers. Sew side and sleeve seams. Sew Trellis piping in place. Sew on beads & feathers.

Argyle with Hearts

Sizes Small (Medium, Large)
Finished Chest Measurement:
42½ (47, 50)"
Full Length: 26½ (28, 30)"
Sleeve Length: 17 (18, 19)"
Sleeve Width: 18½(20½, 22)"

Charts: refer to pages 110–111

Materials
Crucci Sport Crepe
(100% wool, 50gm skein
= approximately 65 yds)
7 skeins color A, Forest
6 skeins color B, Raspberry
5 skeins color C, Navy
6 skeins color D, Rust
Body needle sizes under
Gauge
Rib needle sizes 6, 7, or 9
Size 7, 16" circular needle
Bobbins

Gauge
20 sts and 26 rows = 4" over
colorwork using size 8 needles
or size required to achieve
correct gauge.
18 sts and 24 rows = 4" over
colorwork using size 9 needles
or size required to achieve
correct gauge.
17 sts and 22 rows = 4" over
colorwork using size 10
needles or size required to
achieve correct gauge.

A love for argyles is taken to heart in this sentimental treatment of a conventional form. Delightfully subtle, hearts

offer a graphic contrast with a symbolic message that bears repeating. Bright, bold and flatteringly fun, it is a contemporary break for the wild at heart.

Pattern Stitches
1x1 Corrugated rib
Row 1: (RS) P1A, *p1A, k1B;
rep from*, end p1A.
Row 2: *K1A, p1B; rep from*,
end k2A.
Rows 3 & 4: Rep Rows 1 & 2
changing color B to color D.
Row 5: Rep Row 1 changing
color D to color C. At end
of row, cut C.
Row 6: Rep Row 2 changing
color C to color D.
Row 7: Rep Row 1 using
colors A & D.
Row 8: Rep Row 2 changing
color D to color B.
Row 9: Rep Row 1 using
colors A & B.
1x1 Corrugated rib
(in the round)
Rnd 1: *P1A, k1B; rep
from*.
Rnds 2 – 9: Rep Rnd 1
changing colors as above.
Stockinette stitch
Row 1: (RS) Knit.
Row 2: Purl.
Reverse Stockinette Stitch
Row 1: (RS) Purl.
Row 2: Knit.
Seed stitch
Row 1: (RS) *K1, p1; rep from*.
All subsequent rows - Knit the
purls and purl the knits.

Argyle with Hearts

Intarsia technique (see Knitting Techniques) is used for color blocks. Seed st is used for hearts.

Fair isle technique (see Knitting Techniques) is used for Border chart.

Note
Work individual color blocks with separate bobbins of color. Work all heart motifs in Seed stitch.

Back
With smaller needles and color A, CO 106 sts (all sizes). WS facing, beginning with a knit row, work 3 rows of Rev St st. RS facing, work 9 rows of 1x1 Corrugated rib. Change to larger needles. WS facing and color A, p3 rows. Work 21 rows Border chart. WS facing and color A, p3 rows. Work Back chart to beginning of neck shaping. **Shape neck:** RS facing, work 41 sts in established pattern. Place center 24 sts on hold. Join new yarns. Work 41 sts in established pattern. Working both sides at the same time, at each neck edge on every other row, BO 3 sts twice. Work to end of chart. Place rem 35 shoulder sts on hold.

Front
Work as for Back to Front neck shaping. **Shape neck:** RS facing, work 45 sts in established pattern. Place center 16 sts on hold. Join new yarns. Work 45 sts in established pattern. Working both sides at the same time, at each neck edge on every other row, BO 2 sts 5 times. Work to end of chart. Place rem 35 shoulder sts on hold.

Sleeves
With smaller needles and color A, CO 38 sts (all sizes). WS facing, beginning with a knit row, work 3 rows of Rev St st. RS facing, work 9 rows of 1x1 Corrugated rib. Change to larger needles. WS facing and color A, p3 rows, inc 1 st each end on last row – 40 sts. Work 21 rows Border chart, inc 1 st each end every 4 rows 5 times – 50 sts. WS facing and color A, p3 rows, inc 3 sts on last row – 53 sts. Work Sleeve chart, inc 1 st each side every other row 7 times, then every 4 rows 13 times – 93 sts. Work to end of chart or desired length. BO loosely.

Neck band
Knit shoulder sts of Front and Back tog (see Knitting Techniques). With circular needle and color A, beg at left shoulder, pick up 14 sts along left front neck edge, 16 sts on hold, 14 sts along right front neck edge, 6 sts along right back neck edge, 24 sts on hold and 6 sts along left back neck edge – 80 sts. Place marker. Slip marker on each round. Work 9 rounds of 1x1 Corrugated rib. With A, knit 1 rnd; purl 2 rnds. BO loosely in purl.

Finishing
Measure down 9¼ (10¼, 11)" from shoulder seam on Front and Back. Mark for underarm. Set in sleeves between markers. Sew side and sleeve seams matching patterns.

Zuni

Zuni

Size Small/Medium
Finish Chest Measurement:
46"
Full Length: 32½"
Sleeve Length: 19"
Sleeve Width: 23"

Charts: refer to pages 112–113

Materials
Eagle USA Unique 8 Ply
(100% wool, 50gm skein
= approximately 125 yds)
4 skeins color A, Medoc
4 skeins color B, Petral
5 skeins color C, Purple
4 skeins color D, Princess Blue
3 skeins color E, Old Gold
1 skein color F, Black
Needle size 6 or size
required to achieve correct
gauge
Size 6, 16" circular needle

Gauge
22 sts and 30 rows = 4" over
pattern using larger needles.

Pattern Stitches
Reverse Stockinette Stitch
Row 1: (RS) Purl.
Row 2: Knit.
Seed Stitch
Row 1: (RS) *K1, p1; rep from*.
All subsequent rows - Knit the
purls and purl the knits.

Deep, strong and striking colors form heavily textured layers in a symbolic treatment of African culture. Dancing to a beat from the heart of

darkest Africa, it was inspired by the rich colors and graphics of primitive masks, shields and jewelry. Sure to turn heads with its inventive style, its origin is further defined by a subtle jeweled necklace as a royal tribute to the tribal dressings of African art.

1x1 Corrugated Rib
Row 1: (RS) *K1B, p1D; rep
from*, end k1B.
Row 2: *P1B, k1D; rep from*,
end p1B.
Row 3: Rep Row 1.
Row 4: Rep Row 2, changing
color D to color C.
Rows 5 & 6: Rep Rows 1 & 2
using colors B & C.
Rows 7 & 8: Rep Rows 1 &
2 using colors B & A.
Rows 9 & 10: Rep Rows 1
& 2 using colors B & C.
Rows 11 & 12: Rep Rows 7
& 8.
Rows 13-15: Rep Rows 1-3.
Rows 16-18: Rep Rows 4-6.
Stockinette Stitch
Row 1: (RS) Knit.
Row 2: Purl.
Bobble
[k, p, k, p, k,] in next
stitch; turn, p5; turn, k5,
pass last 4 sts over 5th st
on needle.

Note
Work individual color blocks
with separate bobbins of color.

Back
With smaller needles and color
B, CO 114 sts and work 6
rows of Rev St st. K1 row and
inc 14 sts evenly spaced – 128
sts. Work 1x1 Corrugated rib
for 18 rows. K1 row in color B.
Work Back chart to beginning

Zuni

of neck shaping, inc 1 st on last row of Rev st st panel – 129 sts. **Shape neck**: RS facing, work 43 sts in established pattern. Place center 43 sts on hold. Join new yarns. Work 43 sts in established pattern. Working both sides at the same time, at each neck edge on every other row, BO 2 sts 5 times, then 1 st 4 times. Work to end of chart. Place rem 29 shoulder sts on hold.

Front

Work as for Back to Front neck shaping. **Shape neck**: RS facing, work 48 sts in established pattern. Place center 33 sts on hold. Join new yarns. Work 48 sts in established pattern. Working both sides at the same time, at each neck edge on every row, BO 1 st 5 times, then on every other row, BO 2 sts 5 times, then 1 st 4 times. Work to end of chart. Place rem 29 shoulder sts on hold.

Note

The sleeves, above the Corrugated rib and Bobble panel, are worked in Seed st with Rev St st in between each color change.

Any length alteration may be made in the last Seed st panel.

Sleeves

With smaller needles and color B, CO 58 sts. Work rib as for Back. K1 row B. Change to color C. Work 3 rows St st. **Bobble Row**: K1, *work Bobble, knit 6, rep from* 8 times, end k1. Work 3 rows St st. Cut C. Keeping in pattern and inc as indicated below, join color E; work 2½" Seed st; cut E; join color B; work 3 rows Rev St st; cut B; join color A; work 3" Seed st; cut A; join color B; work 3 rows Rev St st, cut B, join color C; work 4" Seed st; cut C; join color B; work 3 rows St st; cut B; join color D; work 5" Seed st; cut D; join color B; work 3 rows Rev St st, *and at the same time*, inc 1 st each side every other row 9 times, every 4 rows 23 times, then every 6 rows twice – 126 sts. Work to desired length. BO loosely.

Collar

Knit shoulder seams of Front and Back tog. With circular needle and color B pick up and knit 140 sts evenly spaced around neck including sts on hold. Work 2 rows Rev St st.

Work 2 rows St st. Work 3 rows of Circle chart. **Decrease Row**: Dec 1 st between each circle – 126 sts. Work last 4 rows of Circle chart. **Decrease Row**: (k7, k2tog) 14 times – 112 sts. Knit 1 row. Work 2 rows Rev St st dec 2 sts evenly spaced – 110 sts. Work 6 rows Corrugated rib as for Back.

Split neck: Working in established pattern rib 26 sts. BO 3 sts at center front neck – 107 sts. Working back and forth, work rem 11 rows of Corrugated rib as for Back. Cut B. RS facing, join B at center front neck. Pick up and k11 sts along split edge. K1 row to opposite collar edge. Pick up and k11 sts along split edge. Turn. Work 3 rows Rev St st. BO 10 sts, k2tog at center front and continue to BO until 12 sts rem. K2tog at center front and BO rem sts.

Finishing

Measure down 11" from shoulder seam on Front and Back. Mark for underarm. Set in sleeves between markers. Sew side and sleeve seams matching patterns.

Moving Blocks

Moving Blocks

Bold, bright and beautiful blocks of color move about with shifting attitudes in relentless pursuit of style and unrestricted comfort. The luxurious shawl collar adds

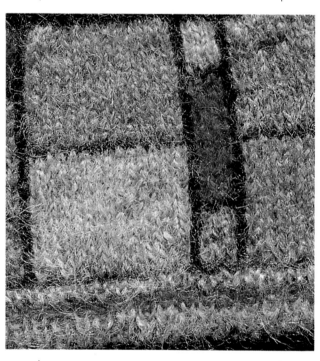

a soft accent to create a classic design boldly in touch with the times. Inspired by the sights and sounds of mid-Manhattan, this is one design that is always on the go.

Sizes Small (Medium, Large)
Finished Chest Measurement:
46 (50, 54)"
Full Length: 27½"
Sleeve Length: 17½"
Sleeve Width: 22"

Charts: refer to pages 114–117

Materials
Crucci Baby Soft Mohair
(80% Mohair, 18% wool,
2% nylon, 50gm skein =
approximately 109 yds)
4 skeins color A, Cyan
4 skeins color B, Cardinal
4 skeins color C, Wilderness
4 skeins color D, Midnight
3 skeins color E, Black
Needle sizes 8 and 10 or
size required to achieve
correct gauge.
Size 10, 24" circular
needle
Bobbins
Four ⅞" buttons

Gauge
16 sts and 20 rows = 4" over
colorwork using larger needles

Pattern Stitches
1x1 Rib
Row 1: (RS) *K1, p1; rep
from*.
Row 2: Knit the knits and purl
the purls.
Stockinette Stitch
Row 1: (RS) Knit.

Row 2: Purl.
Intarsia technique (see Knitting
Techniques) used throughout.

Note
Use bobbins for separate color
blocks and outline stitches
between each block.

Back
With smaller needles and color
E, CO 92 (100, 108) sts.
Work 2 rows each of 1x1
Rib in following color
sequence: colors E, B, D,
C, A, and E. Change to
larger needles. Work Back
chart to beginning of neck
shaping. **Shape neck:**
Work 31 (35, 39) sts in
established pattern. Place
center 30 sts on hold. Join
new yarns. Work 31 (35,
39) sts in established
pattern. Working both
sides at the same time, at
each neck edge on every
other row, BO 2 sts once,
3 sts once, then 2 sts once.
Work to end of chart. Place
rem 24 (28, 32) shoulder sts
on hold.

Left Front
With smaller needles and color
E, CO 41 (45, 49) sts. Work
rib as for Back. Change to
larger needles. Work Left
Front chart to beginning of

neck shaping. **Shape neck:** Dec 1 st on next row once, then every 4 rows 15 times, then every 6 rows once. Work to end of chart. Place rem 24 (28, 32) shoulder sts on hold.

Right Front

Work rib as for Left Front. Work Right Front chart reversing neck shaping.

Sleeves

With smaller needles and color E, CO 36 (40, 40) sts. Work rib as for Back. Change to larger needles. Work Sleeve chart, inc 1 st each end every 2 rows twice, then [every 4 rows twice, every 2 rows once] 5 times, then [every 4 rows once, every 2 rows] twice, then every 2 rows 3 times – 84 (88, 88) sts. Work to end of chart or desired length. BO loosely.

Collar and Front Bands

Knit shoulder sts of Front and Back tog (see Knitting Techniques). With larger needles, color E, and WS of Left Front facing, pick up and purl 56 sts evenly spaced from bottom of rib to beginning of front neck shaping. Cut E. Leave sts on spare double pointed needle and set aside. **Collar:** With color E and circular needle, CO 45 sts.

Cut E. *Join color B. WS facing, work rib over 45 sts. CO 4 sts at end of row. Work rib over 49 sts. CO 4 sts at end of row. Cut B. Join color D. WS facing, work rib over 53 sts. CO 4 sts at end of row. Work rib over 57 sts. CO 4 sts at end of row. Cut D. Join color C. WS facing, work rib over 61 sts. CO 4 sts at end of row. Work rib over 65 sts. CO 4 sts at end of row. Cut C. Join color A. WS facing, work rib over 69 sts. CO 4 sts at end of row. Work rib over 73 sts. CO 4 sts at end of row. Cut A. Join color E. WS facing, work rib over 77 sts. CO 4 sts at end of row. Work rib over 81 sts. CO 4 sts at end of row. Cut E. Rep color sequence from* 4 times and CO 4 sts at the end of each row 20 times total. Continue in color sequence and CO 6 sts at the end of each row 8 times, ending with color A – 173 sts. Cut A. **Join Collar to Front Bands:** Join color E. WS facing, work rib over 173 sts on collar. Pick up and purl 56 sts evenly spaced along WS of Right Front from beginning of front neck shaping to bottom of rib. Turn. Work rib over 229 sts. With RS of Left Front facing, continue rib over 56 sts on double pointed

needle – 285 sts. Cut E. Join color B. Work even in rib over all sts in color B, then color D. Join color C. **Buttonhole Row**: WS facing, work rib over 231 sts, *k2tog, yo, rib 14; rep from* end last rep, rib 4. Work rib in color C over all sts. Cut C. Join color A. Work rib as established. Cut A. Join color E. WS facing, work rib over all sts. Loosely BO 56 sts on Right Front in pattern. Work 173 collar sts in rib. Loosely BO 56 sts on Left Front in pattern. Cut E. Join color E at collar edge. (There are 4 rows of E at center of collar.) WS facing, work even in rib over 173 collar sts in colors E, A, C, D and B. Continue in established color sequence and *at the same time*, dec 6 sts at each end of next 8 rows, then 4 sts at each end of next 20 rows – 45 sts. BO loosely.

Finishing

Fold collar in half lengthwise along center color E rows. Sew in place along neckline. Measure down 10 (10½, 11)" from shoulder seam on Front and Back. Mark for underarm. Set in sleeves between markers. Sew side and sleeve seams matching patterns. Sew on buttons.

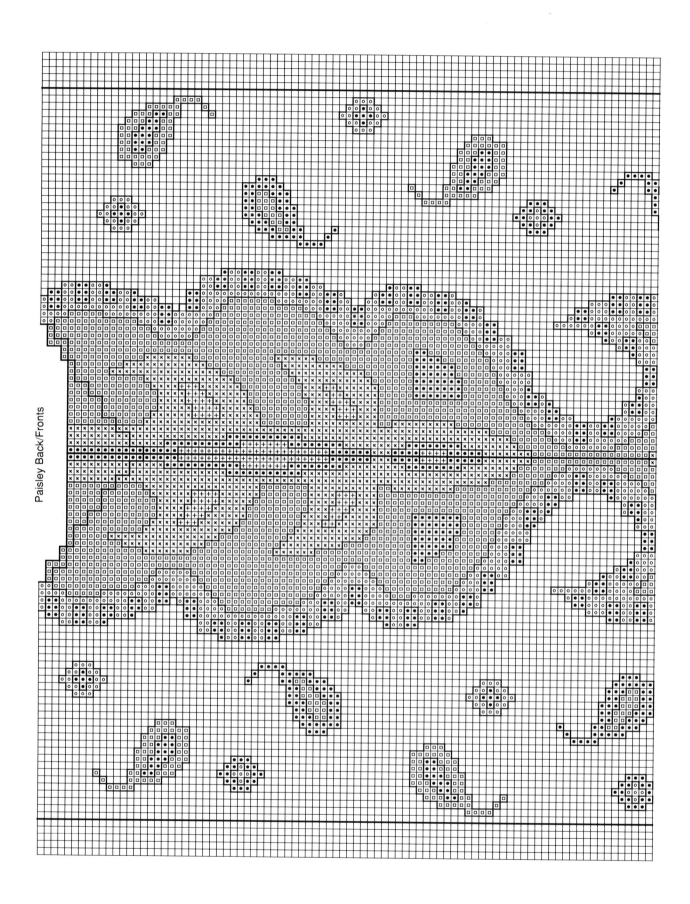

Paisley Back/Fronts

ZUNI

OAK LEAVES

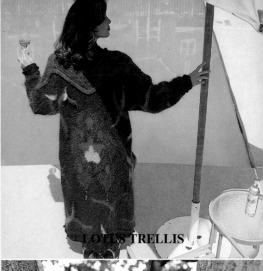

LOTUS TRELLIS

GENTLE MEADOWS

TWO DESIGN PARTNERS FROM
NEW ENGLAND HAVE CREATED
20 ARTISTIC OFFERINGS WITH
UNIQUE STITCHERY DETAIL IN
A FULL COLOR JACKETED HARD
COVER COLLECTOR'S EDITION.

INSPIRING
CAPTIVATING
REWARDING

**KITS AVAILABLE, OF COURSE!
AS SHOWN—OR CUSTOMIZED**

PALEOLITHIC

STAINED GLASS

ARGYLE WITH HEARTS

AZTEC JAZZ

CELESTIAL GARDEN

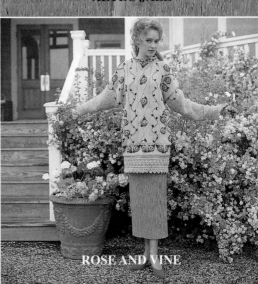

INDIAN SUMMER

ROSE AND VINE

POPPLES AND IRIS

SIGNATURE CARDIGAN

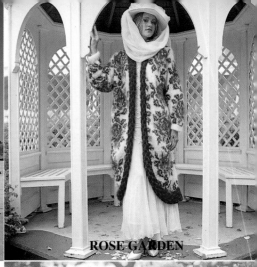

ROSE GARDEN

TARTAN

PAISLEY

DESIGNER ORIGINALS
"ATTENTION TO DETAIL"
THE DK NORTH COLLECTION
DOROTHY T. RATIGAN-KNITTING EDITOR

DRAMATIC
ELEGANT
DISTINCTIVE

PUBLISHED BY EAGLE USA AS
A CONTINUATION OF A FINE SERIES
OF QUALITY HANDKNITTING BOOKS

EAGLE USA

P.O. Box 48282
Seattle, WA
98148

OR AVAILABLE FROM YOUR
LOCAL KNITTING STOCKIST

WILD & WOOLLY STUDIO
7A Meriam Street
Lexington, MA 02173
(617) 861-7717

SHAWL COLLAR CARDIGAN

JEWEL COAT

JESTER

MOVING BLOCKS

CELESTIAL GARDEN

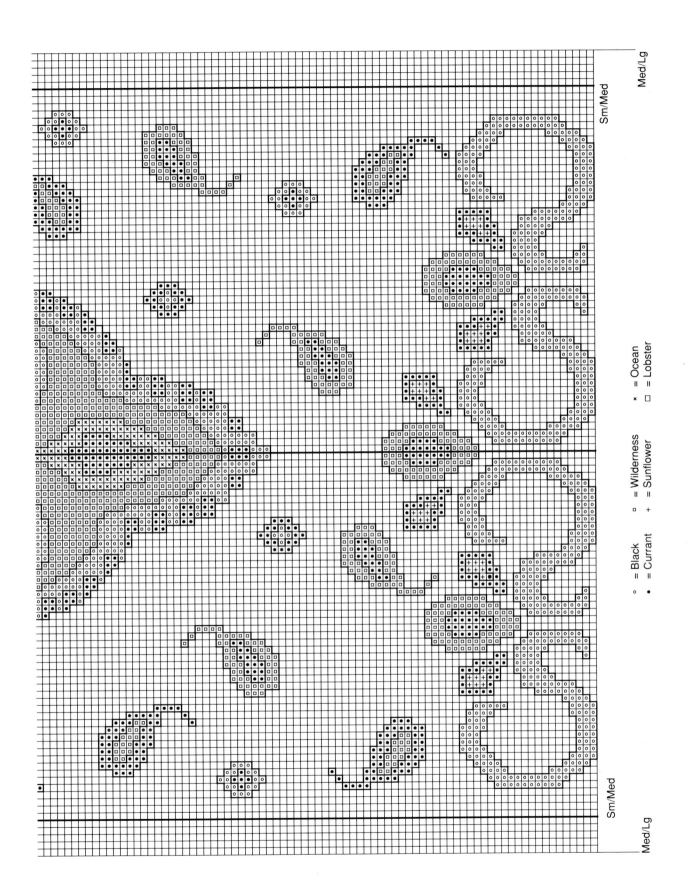

o   = Black   □   = Wilderness   ×   = Ocean
•   = Currant   +   = Sunflower   ◻   = Lobster

Paisley Sleeve

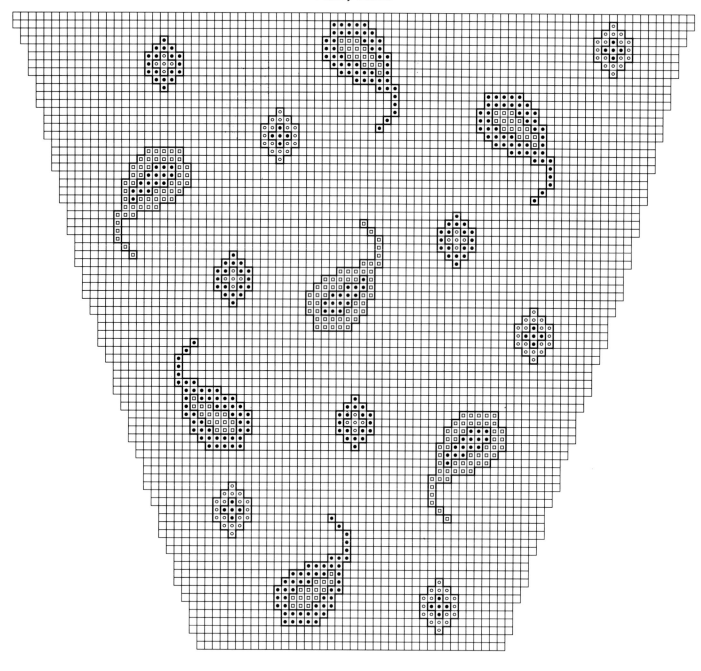

○ = Black   • = Currant   ▫ = Wilderness   ▢ = Lobster

Lotus Trellis Sleeve

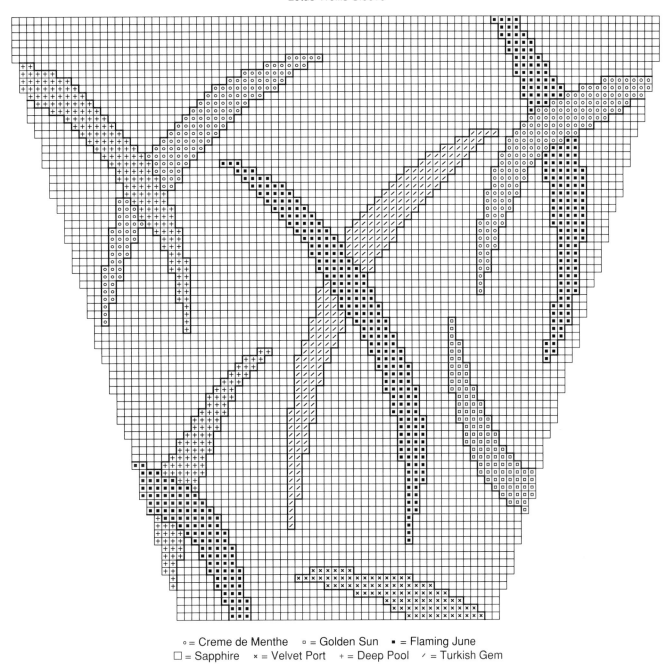

∘ = Creme de Menthe   ▫ = Golden Sun   ▪ = Flaming June

□ = Sapphire   × = Velvet Port   + = Deep Pool   ⁄ = Turkish Gem

One stitch decreased to accomodate pattern.

Lotus Trellis Back

• = Jezabel   ◦ = Creme de Menthe   ▫ = Golden Sun   ▪ = Flaming June   ☐ = Sapphire   × = Velvet Port   + = Deep Pool   ♦ = Wilderness   ✓ = Turkish Gem

☐ = knit on RS; purl on WS   — = purl on RS; knit on WS   ═ = (RS) yarn in back, sl3 sts purlwise. (WS) yarn in front, sl3 sts purlwise. (WS) yarn in back, sl3 sts purlwise.

Lotus Trellis Yoke:

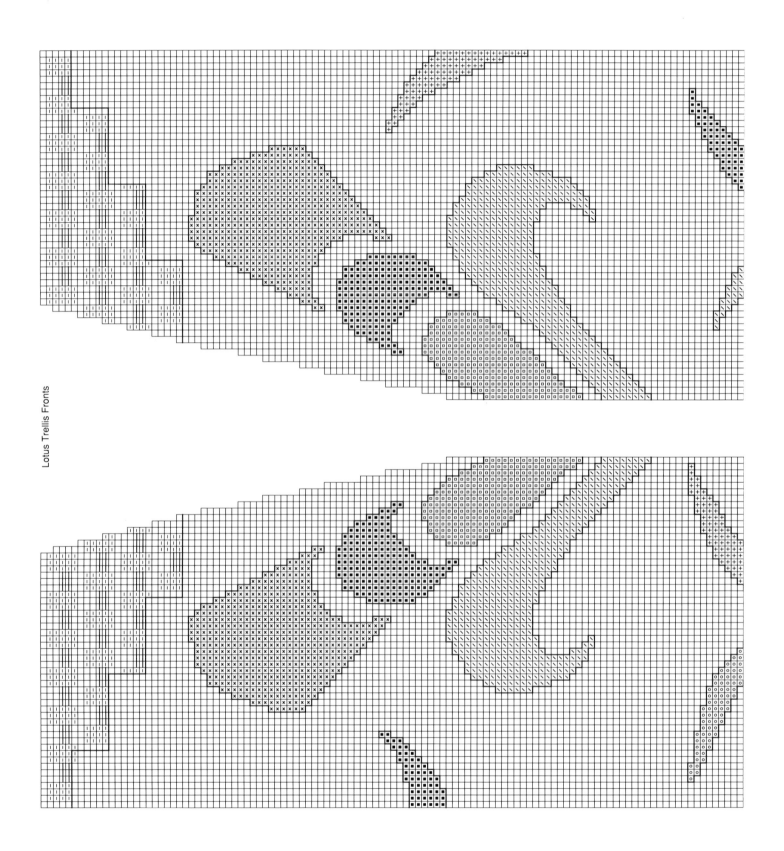

Lotus Trellis Fronts

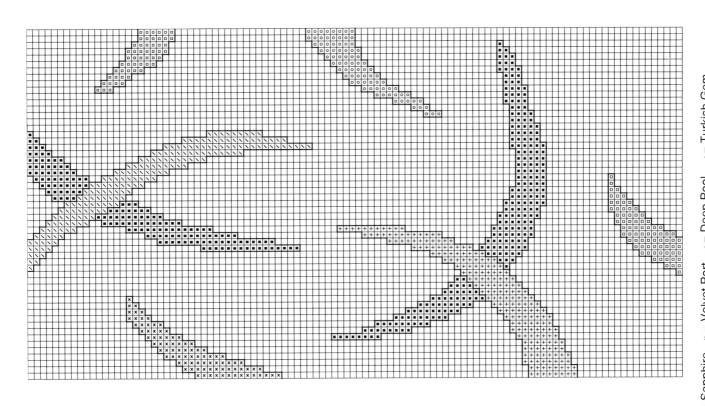

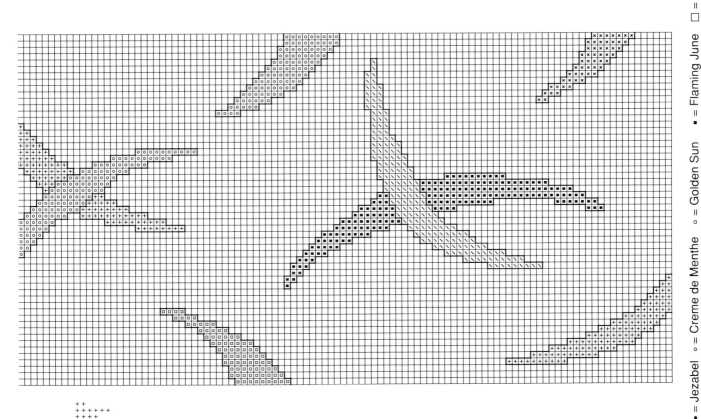

• = Jezabel   ◦ = Creme de Menthe   ▫ = Golden Sun   ■ = Flaming June   □ = Sapphire   × = Velvet Port   + = Deep Pool   ↘ = Turkish Gem

Lotus Trellis Yoke: □ = knit on RS; purl on WS   – = purl on RS; knit on WS   ⫶⫶ = (RS) yarn in front, sl3 sts purlwise. (WS) yarn in back, sl3 sts purlwise.

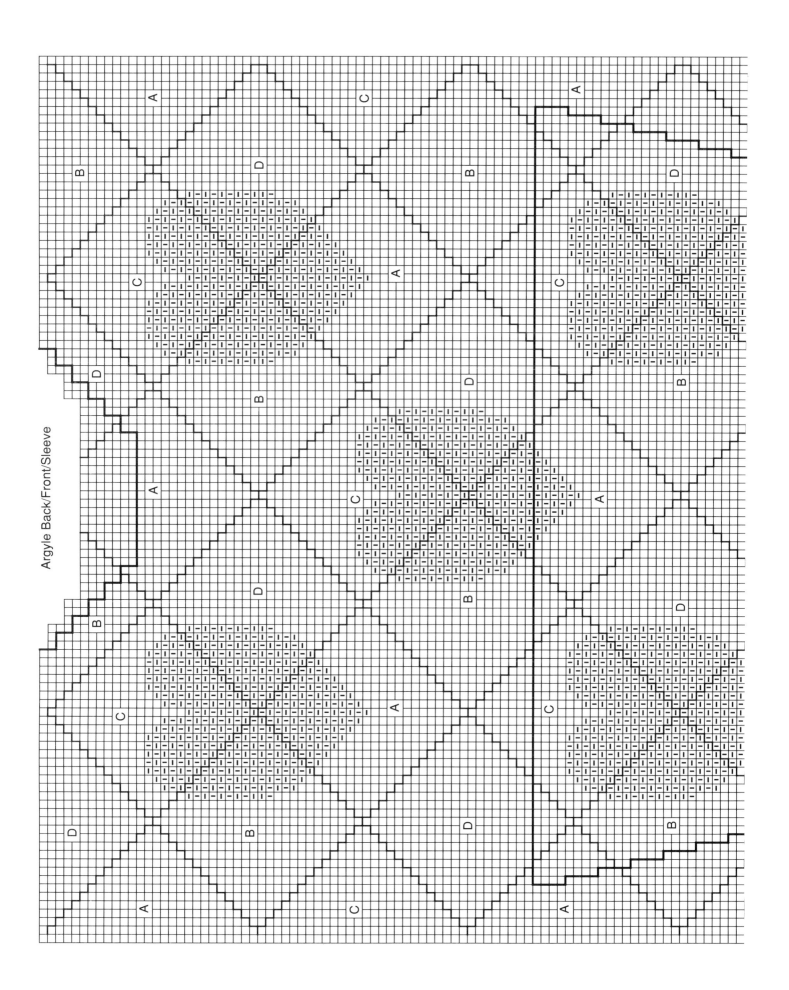

Argyle Back/Front/Sleeve

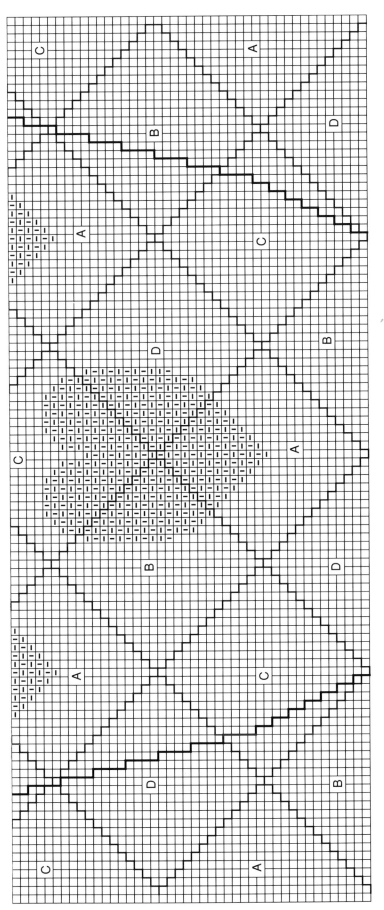

A = Forest   B = Raspberry   C = New York   D = Rust

ı = knit on RS; purl on WS
— = purl on RS; knit on WS

Border Pattern

x = Rust   o = Raspberry   □ = Forest

111

Zuni Back/Front

One stitch increased to accomodate pattern.

Zuni
Circle Chart

Repeat

Begin/end

□ = Purple   v = Petral   • = Princess Blue

x = Sultan   ▨ = knit this st and previous st tog

112

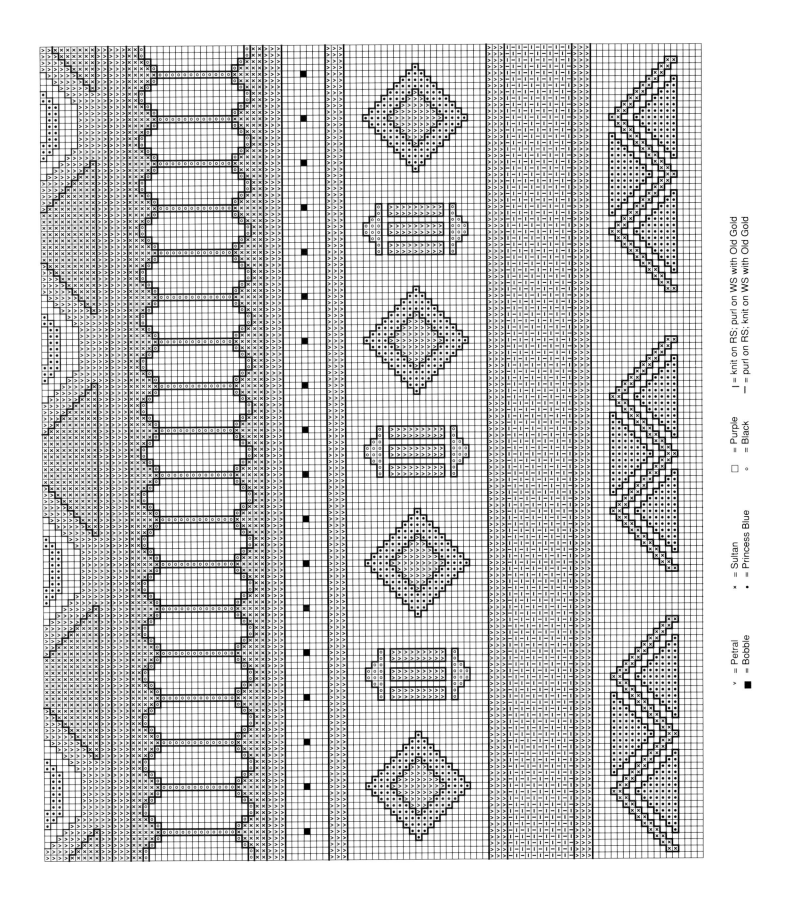

NOTE: Color A "Medoc" is the *same* as "Sultan".

> = Petral   ⌄ = Sultan   □ = Purple   I = knit on RS; purl on WS with Old Gold

■ = Bobble   • = Princess Blue   ○ = Black   — = purl on RS; knit on WS with Old Gold

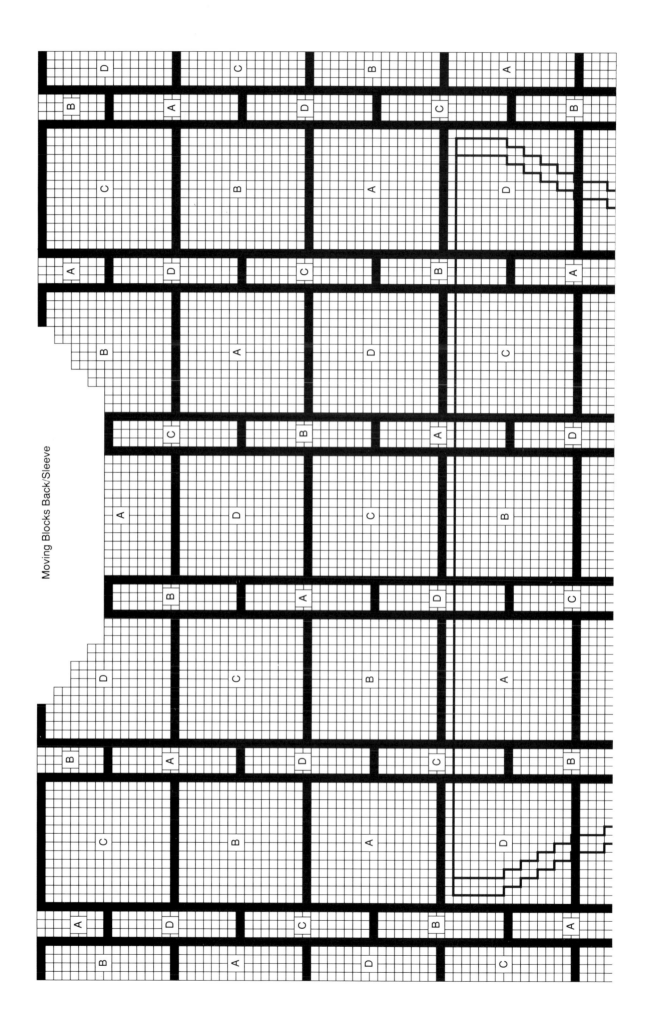

Moving Blocks Back/Sleeve

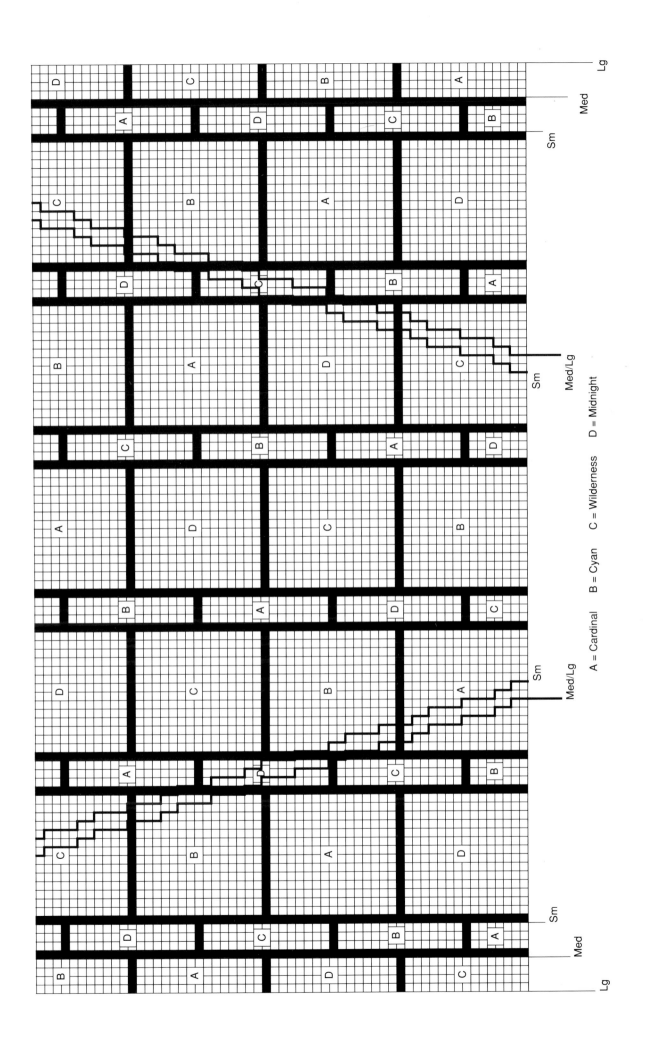

A = Cardinal   B = Cyan   C = Wilderness   D = Midnight

115

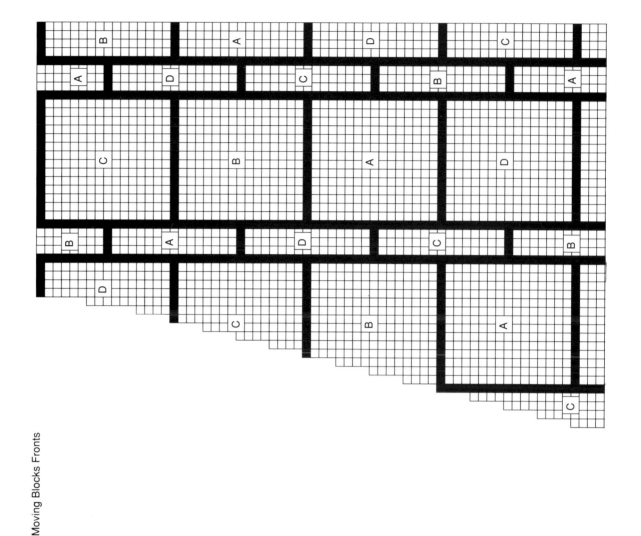

Moving Blocks Fronts

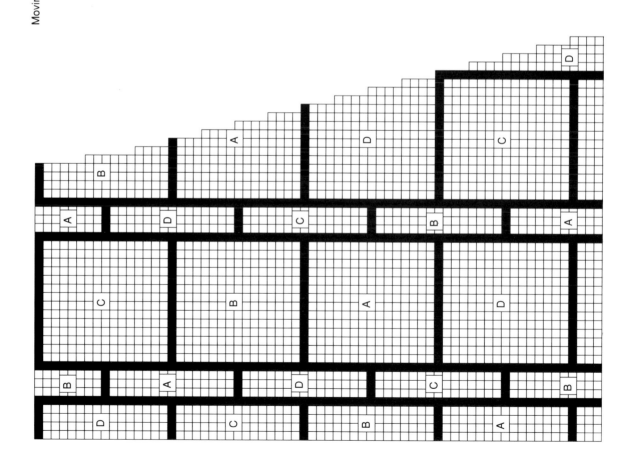

116

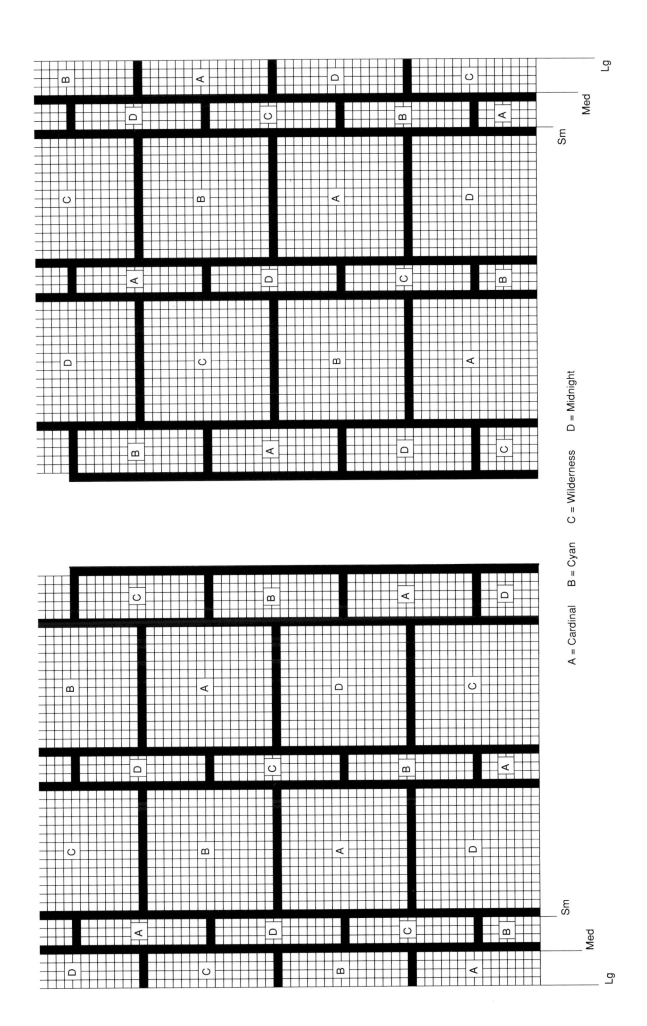

A = Cardinal   B = Cyan   C = Wilderness   D = Midnight

117

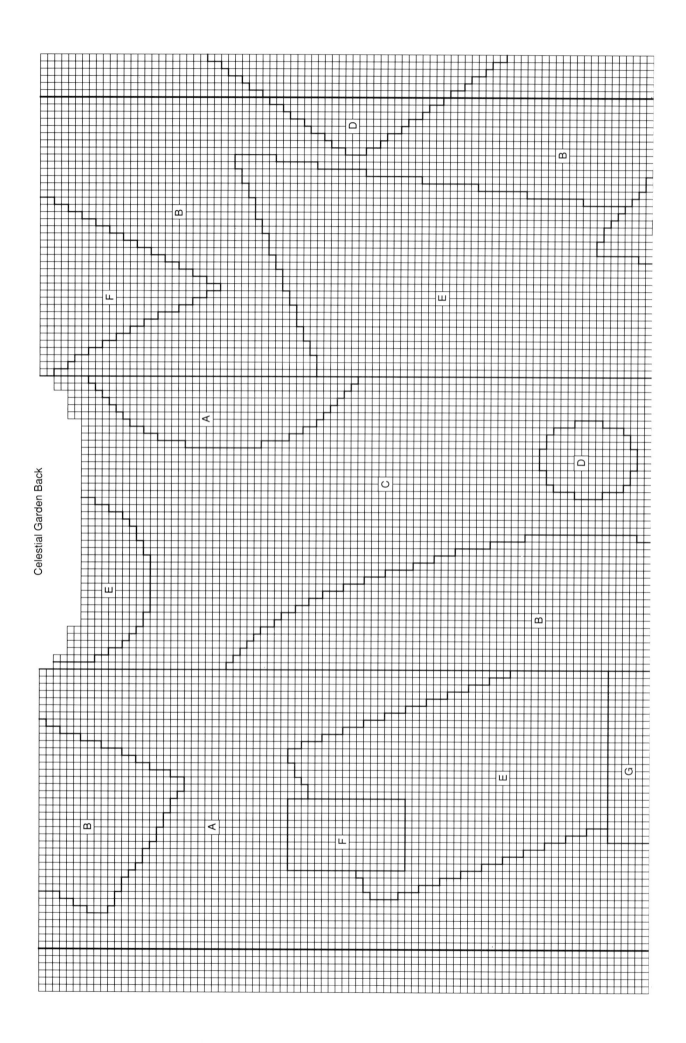

Celestial Garden Back

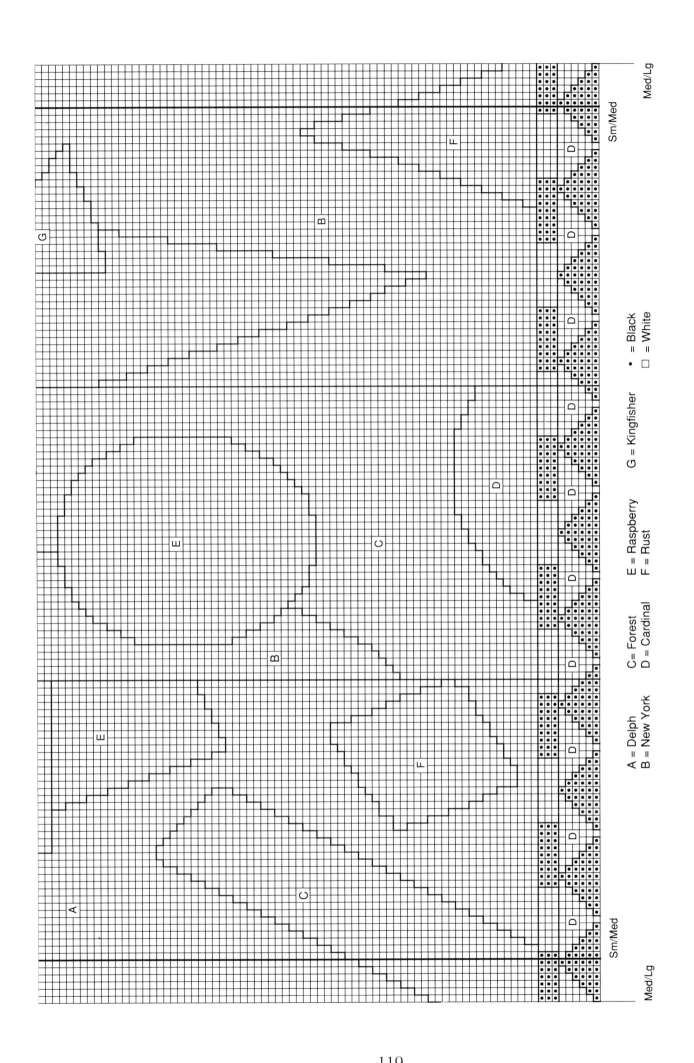

119

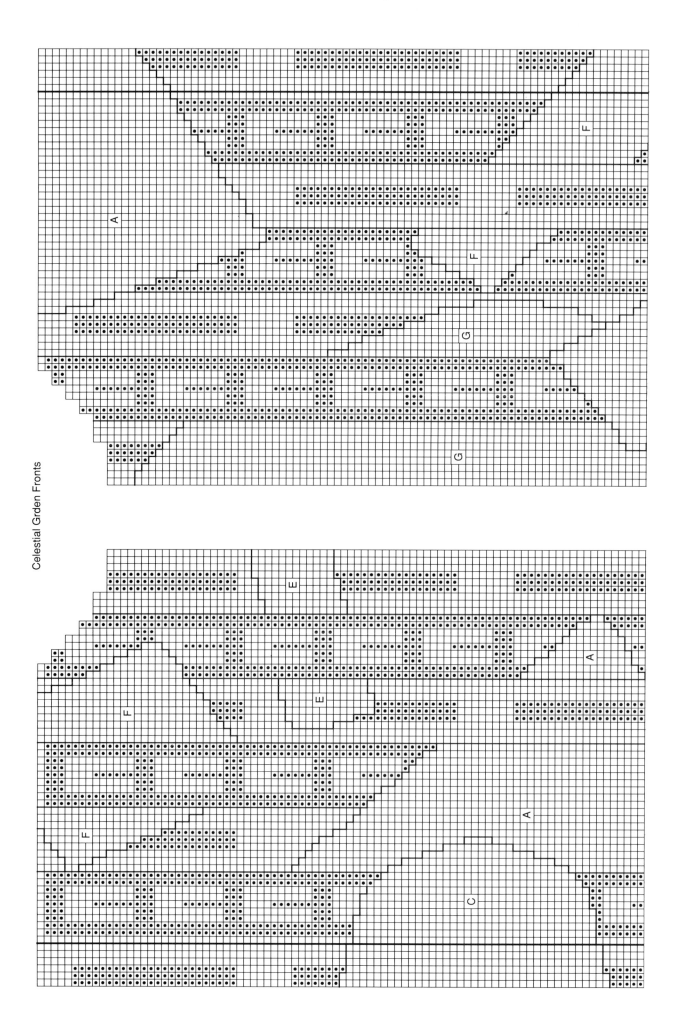

Celestial Grden Fronts

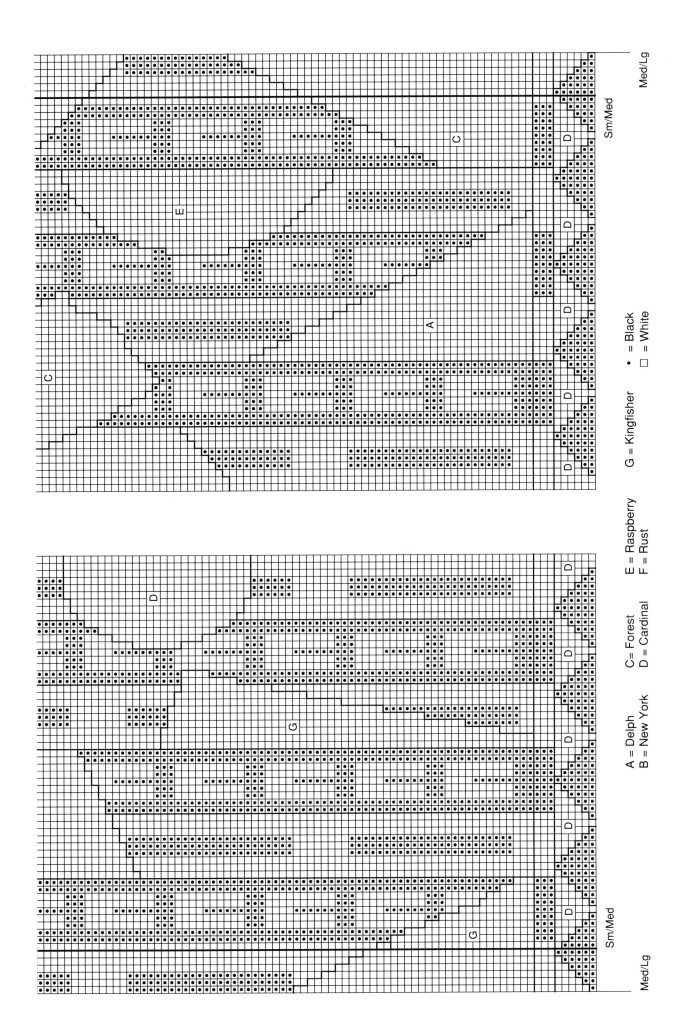

Sm/Med

Med/Lg

Med/Lg

Sm/Med

A = Delph
B = New York

C= Forest
D = Cardinal

E = Raspberry
F = Rust

G = Kingfisher

• = Black
☐ = White

121

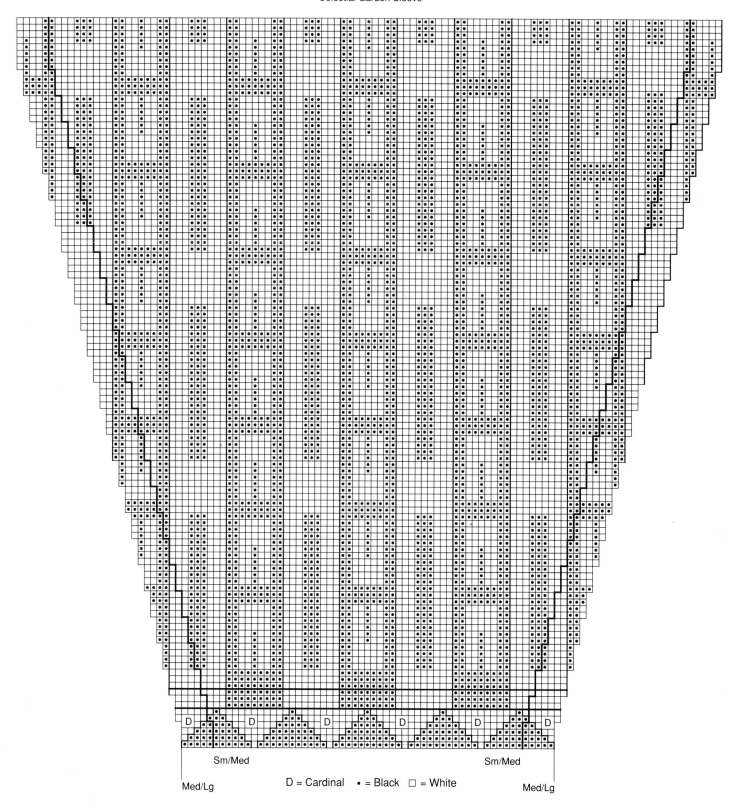

D = Cardinal   • = Black   ☐ = White

Celestial Garden

Celestial Garden

Sizes Small/Medium
(Medium/Large)
Finished Chest Measurement:
43 (47)"
Full Length: 25"
Sleeve Length: 17½"
Sleeve Width: 18 (20)"

Charts: refer to pages 118–122

Materials
Luxury Crepe
(100% Wool, 50gm skein
= approximately 107 yds)
5 skeins White
3 skeins Black
2 skeins color A, Delph
2 skeins color B, New York
2 skeins color C, Forest
1 skein color D, Cardinal
2 skeins color E, Raspberry
1 skein color F, Rust
1 skein color G, Kingfisher
Needle sizes 5 and 6 or
size required to achieve
correct gauge.
Bobbins
Seven ½" buttons

Gauge
22 sts and 30 rows = 4" over
colorwork using larger needles

Random spheres of

color move against a

dark background

reflected by the sun like

celestial bodies floating

through space. Its

colorful lack of tradition

goes perfect with shorts,

jeans or polo players.

Pattern Stitches
1x1 Corrugated rib
Row 1: (RS) *K1D, p1B; rep
from*, end k1D.
Row 2: *P1D, k1B; rep from*,
end p1D.
Stockinette Stitch
Row 1: (RS) Knit.
Row 2: Purl.
Intarsia technique (see Knitting
Techniques) used
throughout.

Note
Work individual color
blocks with separate
bobbins of color.

Back
With smaller needles and
Black, CO 119 (131)
sts. Join color B. Work
1x1 Corrugated rib for
2½". Change to larger
needles. Work Back chart
to beginning of neck
shaping. **Shape neck:** RS
facing, work 45 (51) sts in
established pattern. Place
center 29 sts on hold. Join new
yarns. Work 45 (51) sts in
established pattern.

Working both sides at the same time, at each neck edge on every other row, BO 4 sts once, then 2 sts once. Work to end of chart. Place rem 39 (45) shoulder sts on hold.

Left Front

With smaller needles and Black, CO 55 (61) sts. Work rib as for Back. Change to larger needles. Work Left Front chart to beginning of neck shaping. **Shape neck:** WS facing, BO 6 sts. At neck edge on every other row, BO 4 sts once, then 2 sts 3 times. Work to end of chart. Place rem 39 (45) shoulder sts on hold.

Right Front

Work rib as for Left Front. Work Right Front chart reversing neck shaping.

Sleeves

With smaller needles and Black, CO 49 (59) sts. Work rib as for Back. Change to larger needles. Work Sleeve chart, inc 1 st each end every 4 rows 26 times – 101 (111) sts. Work to end of chart or desired length. BO loosely.

Neck band

Knit shoulder sts of Front and Back tog (see Knitting Techniques). With smaller needles, Black and WS facing, pick up and purl 75 sts around neck. Join color B and work 1x1 Corrugated rib for 1½". BO loosely in Black.

Left Front Border

With smaller needles, Black and WS facing, pick up and purl 143 sts along Left Front edge. Join color B and work 1x1 Corrugated rib for 10 rows. BO loosely in Black.

Right Front Border

Work as for Left Front in Corrugated rib for 4 rows.
Buttonhole row: Beginning at bottom edge, rib 4 sts, *BO 2 sts, rib 20 sts; rep from* end last rep, rib 5 sts. Next row: Working in established pattern, CO 2 sts over BO sts in previous row. Work 4 more rows in Corrugated rib. BO loosely in Black.

Finishing

Measure down 9 (10)" from shoulder seam on Front and Back. Mark for underarm. Set in sleeves between markers. Sew side and sleeve seams matching patterns where possible. Sew on buttons.

Paisley

Paisley

Sizes Small/Medium
(Medium/Large)
Finished Chest Measurement:
53 (58)"
Full Length: 37"
Sleeve Length: 19"
Sleeve Width: 22"

Charts: refer to pages 102–104

Materials
Crucci Baby Soft Mohair
(80% mohair, 18% wool,
2% nylon, 50gm skein =
approximately 109 yds)
8 skeins color A, Lobster
2 skeins color B, Wilderness
2 skeins color C, Currant
1 skein color D, Ocean
1 skein color E, Sunflower
1 skein color F, Black
Kashmir Mohair
(80% wool, 20% mohair,
50gm skein =
approximately 106 yds)
4 skeins color G, Blackberry
Needle sizes 8 and 10 or
size required to achieve correct
gauge.
Bobbins

Gauge
16 sts and 20 rows = 4" over
colorwork using larger needles

This designer virtually throws convention to the wind in a creative illustration of her love for a classic form. In a total flight of fancy, colorful, abstract shapes swirl above the rich accent of a more conventional border.

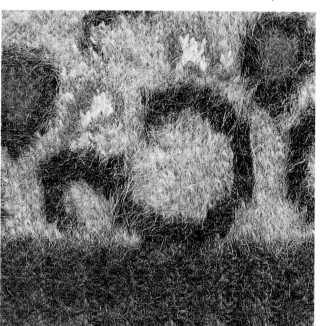

Long, flowing and luxuriously self-indulgent with a royal flare, this magnificent coat immediately communicates a chic self-confidence of style and purpose.

Pattern Stitches
Cabled rib
Row 1: (RS) P2, *k3, p2; rep
from*.
Rows 2 & 4: K2, *p3, k2; rep
from*.
Row 3: P2, *knit the 3rd st,
then knit the 1st and 2nd sts,
p2; rep from*.
Stockinette Stitch
Row 1: (RS) Knit.
  Row 2: Purl.
Intarsia technique (see
Knitting Techniques)
used throughout.

Note
Work individual color
areas with separate
bobbins of color.
Begin Left Front Cabled
rib, with k1, p1 instead of
p2. End Right Front
Cabled rib with p1, k1.
This lends stability to
edge and prevents rolling.

Back
With color G and smaller
needles, CO 102 (112) sts.
Work Cabled rib for 3".
Change to larger needles. Work
Back chart to beginning of
neck shaping. **Shape neck:**
RS facing, work 38 (43) sts in
established pattern. Place

Paisley

center 26 sts on hold. Join new yarns. Work 38 (43) sts in established pattern. Working both sides at the same time, at each neck edge on every other row, BO 2 sts once, then 3 sts once. Work to end of chart. Place rem 33 (38) shoulder sts on hold.

Left Front

With color G and smaller needles CO 67 (72) sts. Work rib as for Back (see Note). Change to larger needles. Work 51 (56) sts of Left Front chart. Place rem 16 sts on hold (front border plus 1 seam st).
Work Left Front to neck shaping. **Shape neck:** WS facing, BO 1 st at neck edge. Work 2 rows, BO 2 sts. On every other row, BO [2 sts, then 3 sts] 3 times. Work to end of chart. Place rem 33 (38) shoulder sts on hold.

Right Front

Work rib as for Left Front (see Note). Work Right Front chart reversing neck shaping.

Sleeves

With color G and smaller needles, CO 40 sts (both sizes). Work rib as for Back. Change to larger needles. Work Sleeve chart, inc 1 st each end [every 2 rows, then every 4 rows] 8 times, every 4 rows 7 times, then every 2 rows once – 88 sts. Work to end of chart or desired length. BO loosely.

Left Front Border

Slip 16 sts to smaller needle. Join color G. Work Cabled rib to beginning of neck shaping. Leave sts on hold. Sew to Left Front along extra seam st.

Right Front Border

Work as for Left Front border ending on same row.

Neck band

Knit shoulder sts of Front and Back tog (see Knitting Techniques). With smaller needles, color G, and RS facing, work across 14 sts of Right Front border in established pattern, p2tog (next st and right front border seam st), pick up and knit 75 sts along neck edge, p2tog(next st and left front border seam st), work 14 sts in established pattern – 105 sts. Work Cabled rib for 2". BO loosely.

Finishing

Measure down 11" (both sizes) from shoulder seam on Front and Back. Mark for underarm. Set in sleeves between markers. Sew side and sleeve seams.

Gentle Meadows

Gentle Meadows

Sizes Small (Medium, Large)
Finished Chest Measurement:
44 (48, 52)"
Full Length: 28"
Sleeve Length: 18 (18½, 19)"
Sleeve Width: 19 (20, 21)"

Charts: refer to pages 132–133

Materials
Eagle USA 8 Ply Perendale
100% wool, 50gm skein =
approximately 108 yds)
16 (18, 20) skeins color A,
Sage
2 (2, 3) skeins color B, Pine
Forest
1 skein color C, Leaf
1 skein color D, Burgundy
1 skein color E, Heather
Needle size 6 or size
required to achieve correct
gauge
Size 7, dpn & 24" circular
needle for Bottom Border
Bobbins

Gauge
22 and 32 rows = 4" over
colorwork using smaller
needles

Pattern Stitches
Cable Definitions
3/3RC
Slip next 3 sts to cn, hold in
back, k3, then k3 on cn.
3/3LC
Slip next 3 sts to cn, hold in
front, k3, then k3 on cn.
C5R
Slip next 3 sts to cn, hold in

*A fresh breeze,
arising from the Irish
Sea, gently floats
across the land,
rejuvenates
its people, awakens
nature's colors and
redefines the landscape.*

*Like the breeze,
"Gentle Meadows",
rejuvenates the artistry
of Aran knitting,
awakens one's
sensibility to color and
design, and redefines
the cable.*

back, k2, purl last st on cn, then
k2 on cn.
C5L
Slip next 3 sts to cn, hold in
front, k2, purl last st on cn, then
k2 on cn.
1/1RC
Slip next st to cn, hold in back,
k1, then p1 on cn.
1/1LC
Slip next st to cn, hold in front,
p1, then k1 on cn.
1/2PRC
Slip next 2 sts to cn, hold
in back, k1, then p2 on cn.
1/2PLC
Slip next st to cn, hold in
front, p2, then k1 on cn.
2/1RC
Slip next st to cn, hold in
back, k2, then p1 on cn.
2/1LC
Slip next 2 sts to cn, hold
in front, p1, then k2 on cn.
Bobble
(k1, p1, k1, p1, k1, p1, k1)
all in next st. Pass the 2nd,
3rd, 4th, 5th, 6th and 7th
sts over the first st.
2/2RC
Slip next 2 sts to cn, hold in
back, k2, then k2 on cn.

Bottom Border
With 24" circular needle and
color B, CO 285 (310, 335) sts.
Join, being careful not to twist sts.
Rnd 1: (RS) *yo, k5, lift 2nd,
3rd, 4th, and 5th sts over the
first st; rep from*.
Rnd 2: *K1, (k1, yo, k1b) in next
st; rep from*.

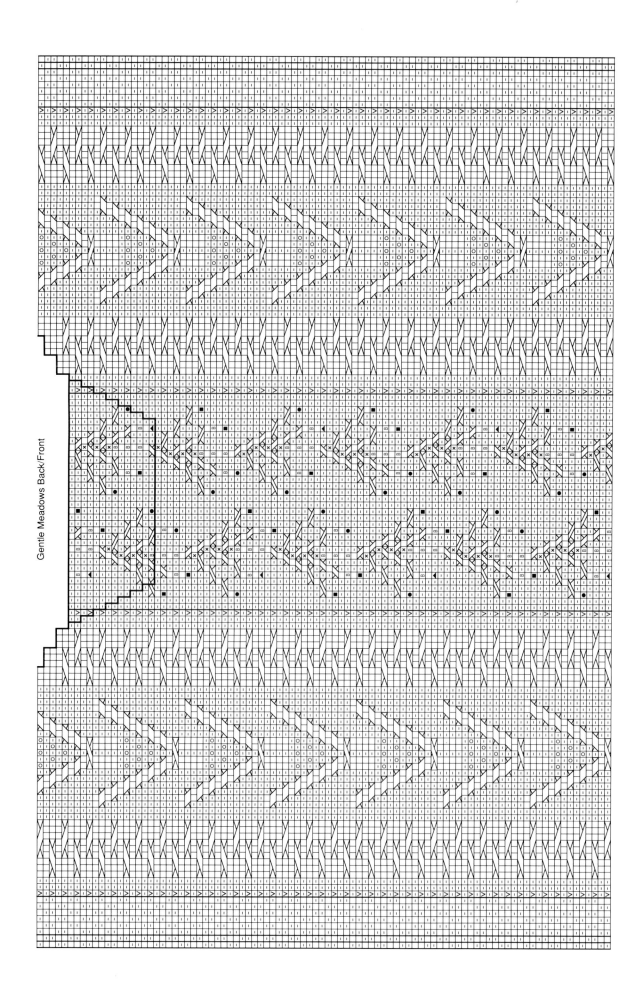

Gentle Meadows Back/Front

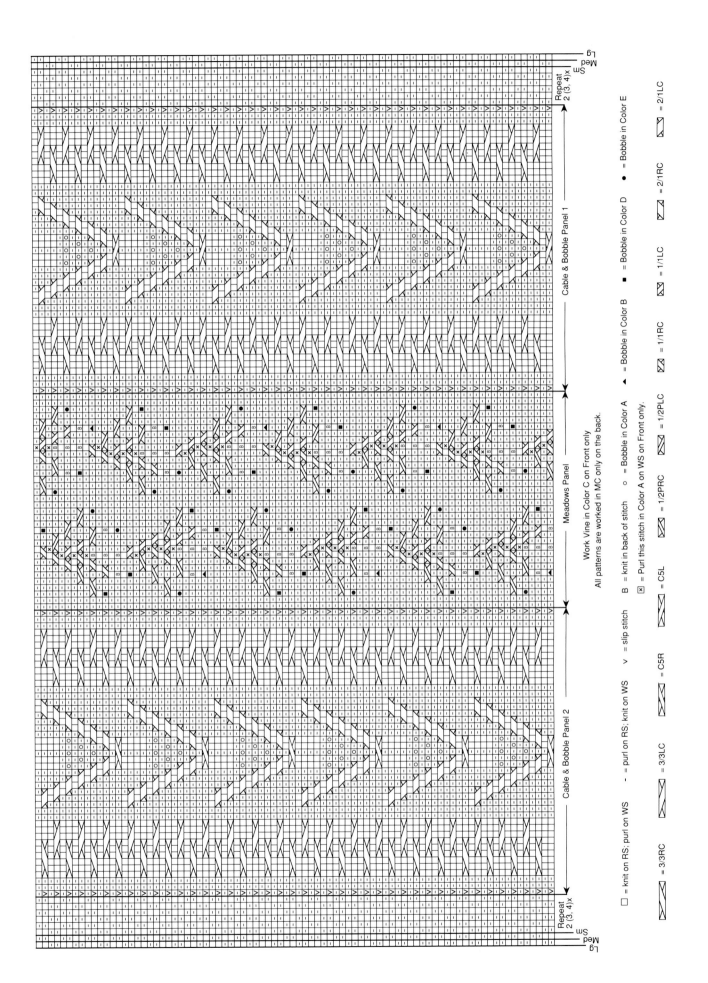

Repeat 2 (3, 4)x

Sm
Med
Lg

Cable & Bobble Panel 1

Meadows Panel

Work Vine in Color C on Front only
All patterns are worked in MC only on the back.

Cable & Bobble Panel 2

Repeat 2 (3, 4)x

Sm
Med
Lg

□ = knit on RS; purl on WS

- = purl on RS; knit on WS

v = slip stitch

B = knit in back of stitch

⊠ = Purl this stitch in Color A on WS on Front only.

☒ = Purl this stitch in Color A on WS on Front only.

o = Bobble in stitch

o = Bobble in Color A

◀ = Bobble in Color B

■ = Bobble in Color D

● = Bobble in Color E

⬚ = 1/2PLC

⬚ = 1/1RC

⬚ = 1/1LC

⬚ = 2/1RC

⬚ = 2/1LC

⬚ = C5L

⬚ = 1/2PRC

⬚ = C5R

⬚ = 3/3LC

⬚ = 3/3RC

133

Rnd 3: *K3, (k1b, p1) in next st; rep from*.
Rnd 4: Purl.
Rnd 5: Knit and inc 1 (2, 3) sts evenly spaced along last rnd.
Rnd 6: *P1, (k1, yo) twice, k2, mB (make Bobble), k4, ssk, sl1, k2 tog, psso, k2tog, k4, mB, k2, (yo, k1) twice; rep from* 11 (12, 13) times.
Rnds 7, 9, 11, 13 & 15: Knit.
Rnd 8: *P1, k1, (k1, yo) twice, k2, mB, k3, ssk, sl1, k2 tog, psso, k2tog, k3, mB, k2, (yo, k1) twice, k1; rep from* 11 (12, 13) times.
Rnd 10: *P1, mB, k1, (k1, yo) twice, k2, mB, k2, ssk, sl1, k2 tog, psso, k2tog, k2, mB, k2, (yo, k1) twice, k1, mB; rep from* 11 (12, 13) times.
Rnd 12: *P1, k1, mB, k1, (k1, yo) twice, k2, mB, k1, ssk, sl1, k2 tog, psso, k2tog, k1, mB, k2, (yo, k1) twice, k1, mB, k1; rep from* 11 (12, 13) times.
Rnd 14: *P1, k2, mB, k1, (k1, yo) twice, k2, mB, ssk, sl1, k2 tog, psso, k2tog, mB, k2, (yo, k1) twice, k1, mB, k2; rep from* 11 (12, 13) times.
Rnd 16: *P1, k3, mB, k1, (k1, yo) twice, k2, ssk, sl1, k2 tog, psso, k2tog, k2, (yo, k1) twice, k1, mB, k3; rep from* 11 (12, 13) times. K1 rnd, p1 rnd, k1 rnd. BO all sts. Set aside.

Large Border Cable (16 sts)

Rows 1, 3 & 7: (RS) Sl1, (k1, p1) twice, k6, (p1, k1) twice, p1.
Row 2 and all WS rows: (P1, k1) twice, k1, p6, k1, (k1, p1) twice.
Row 5: Sl1, (k1, p1) twice, 3/3RC, (p1, k1) twice, p1.

Moss Stitch

Row 1: *K1, p1; rep from*.
Rows 2 & 4: Knit the knits and purl the purls.
Row 3: *P1, k1; rep from*.

Cable & Bobble Panel 1 (45 sts)

Row 1: (RS) Sl1, p2, k9, p8, C5L, p8, k9, p2, sl1.
Row 2 and all even rows: Knit the knits and purl the purls.
Row 3: Sl1, p2, 3/3LC, k3, p7, 2/1RC, p1, 2/1LC, p7, k3, 3/3RC, p2, sl1.
Row 5: Sl1, p2, k3, 3/3RC, p6, 2/1RC, p1, mB, p1, 2/1LC, p6, 3/3LC, k3, p2, sl1.
Row 7: Sl1, p2, 3/3LC, k3, p5, 2/1RC, (p1, mB) twice, 2/1LC, p5, k3, 3/3RC, p2, sl1.
Row 9: Sl1, p2, k3, 3/3RC, p4, 2/1RC, (p1, mB) 3 times, 2/1LC, p4, 3/3LC, k3, p2, sl1.
Row 11: Sl1, p2, 3/3LC, k3, p3, 2/1RC, p2, k2, p1, k2, p2, 2/1LC, p3, k3, 3/3RC, p2, sl1.
Row 13: Sl1, p2, k3, 3/3RC, p2, 2/1RC, p3, k2, p1, k2, p3, 2/1LC, p2, 3/3LC, k3, p2, sl1.

Cable & Bobble Panel 2 (45 sts)

Row 1: (RS) Sl1, p2, k9, p8, C5R, p8, k9, p2, sl1.
Rows 2-14: Work as for Cable & Bobble Panel 1.

Meadows Panel (34 sts)

Row 1: P6, 1/1LC, 1/1RC, p1, 1/2PRC, p7, k1B, p2, k1B, p3, mB, p5.
Row 2 and all even rows: Knit the knits and purl the purls.
Row 3: P7, 1/1LC, 1/2PRC, p6, mB, p2, 1/1LC, p1, k1b, p3, k1b, p5.
Row 5: P8, 1/1LC, p2, mB, p5, 1/2PLC, p1, 1/1LC, k1b, p1, 1/2PRC, p2, mB, p2.
Row 7: P5, mB, p3, k1b, p2, k1b, p7, 1/2PLC, 1/1LC, 1/1RC, p2, 1/2PRC, p2.
Row 9: P5, k1b, p3, k1b, p1, 1/1RC, p2, mB, p6, 1/1LC, 1/1RC, p1, 1/2PRC, p4.
Row 11: P2, mB, p2, 1/2PLC, p1, k1b, 1/1RC, p1, 1/2PRC, p7, 1/1LC, 1/2PRC, p6.
Row 13: P2, 1/2PLC, p2, 1/1LC, 1/1RC, 1/2PRC, p10, 1/1LC, p2, mB, p5.
Row 15: P4, 1/2PLC, p1, 1/1LC, 1/1RC, p9, mB, p3, k1b, p2, k1b, p5.
Row 17: P6, 1/2PLC, 1/1RC, p10, k1b, p3, k1b, p1, 1/1RC, p2, mB, p2.
Row 19: P5, mB, p2, 1/1RC, p8, mB, p2, 1/2PLC, p1, k1b, 1/1RC, p1, 1/2PRC, p2.
Row 21: P5, k1b, p2, k1b, p3, mB, p5, 1/2PLC, p2, 1/1LC, 1/1RC, 1/2PRC, p4.
Row 23: P2, mB, p2, 1/1LC, p1, k1b, p3, k1b, p7, 1/2PLC, p1, 1/1LC, 1/1RC, p6.
Row 25: P2, 1/2PLC, p1, 1/1LC, k1b, p1, 1/2PRC, p2, mB, p6, 1/2PLC, 1/1RC, p7.
Row 27: P4, 1/2PLC, 1/1LC, 1/1RC, p2, 1/2PRC, p5, mB, p2, 1/1RC, p8.

Gentle Meadows

Stockinette Stitch
Row 1: (RS) Knit.
Row 2: Purl.

Small Cuff Cable (8 sts)
Rows 1 & 3: Sl1, p1, k4, p1, sl1.
Row 2 and all even rows: P1, k1, p4, k1, p1.
Row 5: Sl1, p1, 2/2RC, p1, sl1.

Neck band Cable (11 sts)
With smaller needles and Color A, CO 11 sts.
Rows 1, 3 & 7: K6, (p1, k1) twice, sl1.
Rows 2 & 4: P1, k1, p1, k2, p6.
Row 5: 3/3 RC, (p1, k1) twice, sl1. Work Neck band Cable for 16". BO all sts.

Notes
The Bottom Border is worked circularly. This allows a center pointelle to be aligned under the Meadows Panel.
Back and Front are worked separately.
Slip all sts as if to knit.

Back
With smaller needles and color A, CO 16 sts. Rep 8 rows of Large Border Cable for 44 (48, 52)". BO on Row 8. Seam ends. Fold in half with seam at center back. Mark for side seams. With Color A, smaller needles, and WS facing, pick up 148 (162, 176) sts along slip st back edge between markers. Work Back chart to beginning of neck shaping. **Shape neck:** RS facing, work 54 (61, 68) sts in established pattern. Place center 40 sts on hold. Join new yarn. Work 54 (61, 68) sts in established pattern. Working both sides at the same time, at each neck edge on every other row, BO 3 sts twice. Work to end of chart. Place rem 48 (55, 62) shoulder sts on hold.

Front
Work as for Back to beginning of Front neck shaping. **Shape neck:** RS facing, work 61 (68, 75) sts in established pattern. Place center 26 sts on hold. Join new yarn. Work 61 (68, 75) sts in established pattern. Working both sides at the same time, at each neck edge on every other row, BO 1 st 7 times, then 3 sts twice. Work to end of chart. Place rem 48 (55, 62) shoulder sts on hold.

Right Sleeve
With dpn and color B, CO 80 sts (all sizes). Join. Work Rnds 1-4 of Bottom Border. Knit 1 rnd and BO all sts. Set aside. With smaller needles and color A, CO 16 sts (all sizes). Work Large Border Cable as for Back for 11". Do not break yarn. With WS facing, pick up 44 sts along slip st edge. Work in St st for 14 rows, inc 1 st on each edge every 4 rows 3 times – 50 sts. BO all sts. Set aside. With smaller needles and color A, CO 8 sts (all sizes). Work Small Cuff Cable for 10" ending on Row 6.

Do not break yarn. With WS facing, pick up 71 sts along slip st edge. Work 13 Moss sts, 45 sts in Cable & Bobble Panel 1, work 13 Moss sts. Inc 1 st each end in pattern every other row 0 (4, 8) times, then every 4 rows 26 (26, 25) times – 123 (131, 137) sts. Work to 18 (18½, 19)" or desired length. BO loosely.

Left Sleeve
Work as for Right Sleeve substituting Cable & Bobble Panel 2 for Panel 1.
Knit shoulder sts of Front and Back tog (see Knitting Techniques).

Finishing
Measure down 9½ (10, 10½)" from shoulder seam on Front and Back. Mark for underarm. Set in sleeves between markers. Loosely sew Neck band Cable to neckline. Sew Bottom Border to Large Border Cable centering pointelle. Work Chain Stitch and French Knots (see Knitting Techniques) on St st panel on both sleeves. Sew St st panel to Small Cuff Cable. Sew small Bottom Border to Large Border Cable on both sleeves. Sew side and sleeve seams.

Alternate color choices for garment:
Color A: Bleach/Soft Pink/Silver/Vanilla
Color B: Bayou/Teal/Black/Earth
Color C: Sea Spray/Leaf/Dk Grey/Muffin
Color D: Electric Blue/Burgundy/
Electric Blue/Rust
Color E: Mauve/Ruby/Pink/Flame

Acknowledgments

Original Book Design Kim Barry
Book Layout & Pattern Graphics Kim Barry and Dorothy T. Ratigan
Project Coordinator Diane Lincoln

With the exception of "Gentle Meadows" design
Photography Elizabeth Proulx • *Copy* Rick Small
Hair & Make-up Karen Haas and Maureen Sanford
Styling Rick Small and Diane Lincoln
Models Stacy Teas, Sabra Joselyn

Photography on location at Inn By the Sea
and Fort Williams Park, both in Cape Elizabeth, Maine

*We are grateful to the following Maine companies
for providing apparel, and accessories for photography*
Joseph's of Portland • Dino International Furs of South Portland
Tavecchia of Portland • Queen of Hats of Portland
Howard's Leather Clothing and Boot Co. of Yarmouth
Carla Bella of Portland, and Parade of Shoes of South Portland

*A big Thank You to all the knitters and finishers
who spent so many hours knitting our designs*

Wendy Fisher • Mary Harmon • Sandy Uhlig • Dorothy T. Ratigan
Ann Largay • Patty Lincoln • Elizabeth Proulx • Cathy Bisson
Ida Soucier • Deedra Dapice • Nellie Karpowich • Mary Merrill
Carol Philbrook and LVZ

We would also like to express our warmest affection to our families and friends,
particularly, to our parents Patty Lincoln, and Susan and Richard Barry
for their encouragement and support throughout this project.

A special dedication is made to our editor and mentor,
Dorothy T. Ratigan, for her personal interest in our project,
her guidance, her technical expertise in translating our patterns,
her help and advice throughout this project, and the contribution of
her original design "Gentle Meadows." Thank you!!!

"Gentle Meadows" was modeled by Heather Vermef at Puget Sound,
Seattle, Washington with photography by Robert Palon of Expertography.

Finally, we extend our gratitude to George and Jinx Vermef
without whom this book would not be published.